NOW I CAN THINK MYSELF TO MARS

Second Edition

(Ten Bonus Journal Entries)

NOW I CAN THINK MYSELF TO MARS: TEN BONUS JOURNAL ENTRIES
Copyright © 2024 2nd Edition by Grace Hournbuckle Walker

Library of Congress Control Number: 2024904737

ISBN	Paperback:	979-8-89091-481-1
ISBN	Hardback:	979-8-89091-686-0
ISBN	eBook:	979-8-89091-482-8

Includes the following 3 previously copyrighted works by author. Bedtime Prayer of a Warrior King and 3 other Unpublished works: Bedtime Prayer of a Warrior King, Lament of a Tarnished Vessel, Remember the Potter
Registration Number TXU002353505 Date 2022-12-21
Copyright © 2022 Grace Hournbuckle Walker

All rights reserved. No part of this book may be used or reproduced by any means, graphic, electronic, or mechanical, including photocopying, recording, taping or by any information storage retrieval system without the written permission of the author except in the case of brief quotations embodied in critical articles and reviews.

NCV scripture taken from the New Century Version®. Copyright © 2005 by Thomas Nelson. Used by permission. All rights reserved.

Scripture quotations marked (NIV) are taken from the Holy Bible, New International Version®, NIV®. Copyright © 2011 by Biblica, Inc. TM Used by permission of Zondervan. All rights reserved worldwide. www.zondervan.com. NIV and New International Version are trademarks registered in the United States Patent and Trademark Office by Biblica, Inc. TM

Scripture quotations marked MSG are taken from The Message, copyright c 1993, 2002, 2018 by Eugene H. Peterson. Used by permission of NavPress. All rights reserved. Represented by Tyndale House Publishers.

Scripture taken from the New King James Version®. Copyright © 1982 by Thomas Nelson. Used by permission. All rights reserved.

Now I Can Think Myself to Mars

Second Edition

(Ten Bonus Journal Entries)

GRACE HOURNBUCKLE WALKER

ReadersMagnet, LLC

Professional Reviews

Sometimes you read a book and you know you're holding something different in your hands. This book isn't one to be read quickly or taken lightly. It is the kind of story that will stay with you long after you've read the last page; it's a special book that you will think of often in the days to come. It's a unique type of book that causes you to measure your own life and experiences thus causing a change in how you look at the world. In this book, author Grace Hournbuckle Walker takes words on a page and causes them to become three dimensional, turning those black scratch marks into virtual arrows that will pierce your heart with every page.

Walker's book is the very model of bibliotherapy; both for the writer and for the reader. Walker wrote *Now I Can Think Myself to Mars* after her young son died of a freak medical occurrence. This book was the pathway for Walker through her grieving, revealing the healing process subliminally on every page. For those who have suffered such a loss, or any epic loss, reading this story will both torment and soothe. It is though, a healthy process of finding solid emotional footing after enduring a tragedy.

The narrative is actually a mixture of letters to Walker's son Nathan after his death and poems using Nathan's own words and other memories from a mother about her silly and warm-hearted child. The poems are organized around the last few days Walker had with her son, who showed no real signs of the impending medical crisis that would end his life. While he had some health problems, if you didn't know how the story was going to end, you would be shocked at the suddenness of it. I think setting up the story in this way led a poignancy of the actual accounts and made every word so very important. Other poems focus on the small moments of a brief life, made even more important due to the brevity.

Throughout the story, Walker leans heavily upon her Christian faith. Each letter and poem focus on how Walker used scripture to overcome dark moments to find her inner strength and sustenance. Most amazing though, is the peace that seems to flow through Walker's words as she wrote about her faith. It sometimes seems as if she is just catching him up on stuff before they meet again in the hereafter.

Walker's book is not to be read easily or plowed through quickly. It's a story that will pull apart your soul, but then will also show how to put it back together again. For anyone who has undergone such a tragedy, it's also a textbook of how writing can help to overcome our deepest sorrows and pain. I would recommend that this book be given as a gift to those going through similar situations as well as a book that can be referred to again and again. *Now I Can Think Myself to Mars: A Son's Final Goodbye, A Mother's Journal of Renewal* can help you endure your own life heartaches.

While no one would wish for this occurrence on anyone, readers can take some comfort in knowing the life of Nathan Walker will enrich your soul. Consider this book a gift from him for having noticed the smaller things in life and for becoming the messenger for others to enjoy a richer life.

Five Star Gold Review
C. C. Thomas
Pacific Book Review

"The loss of you in our lives, Nathan, was more like a hurricane force threatening to throw us off our spiritual course. However, with the peace of God in my heart and faith in his faithfulness, I know there are still good works for me to do here on earth."

This is a mother's creative memorial to her son, Nathan, who died in 1992 not long before his ninth birthday, with no forewarning, from a twisted blood vessel in his abdomen. About a year later, the author, a nurse practitioner and educator, wrote down a phrase that reminded her of him: "Mom, remember when I could travel so fast on my bike…? Now I can think myself to Mars!" This "Remember when/Now I…" format became the basis of poems about Nathan's impact on the family while alive and after he passed on. Walker "talks" to Nathan as she writes, assuming he is in heaven, can "see" and "hear" her, and will be there waiting for her when she dies. She tells Nathan about the later death of his father and her own recent struggles with recovering from an auto accident. Among her poems and spiritual reflections, she has placed her husband's poems, revealing his private search for the meaning of his son's death.

Now retired from her nursing career, Walker still seeks comfort and comprehension by analyzing Nathan's life, death, and afterlife. Her poetry underscores her conviction that he is "in the arms of Jesus," and swims "in the river of life." In her journal entries, the author copes with life's pains by ascribing deeper meaning. Once, stopping in the desert after driving the wrong way, she speaks to her son, alluding to Biblical verses in which the desert is an allegory for our earthly journey. Though not a practiced writer when she began her book, the author grows into the role, offering poignant insights. A book for people experiencing loss, and especially the loss of a child, Now I Can Think Myself to Mars is a gentle guidebook, presenting new paths to process their experience.

Barbara Bamberger Scott
US Review of Books

Heaven is hardly ever on the minds of modern people and it's indicative of Christians also. The story in this book, however, is about how Heaven became very real for a little boy and a mother, and the comfort that they gleaned from Christ as she attended her dying little boy. This book is a tender read and very moving. It reflects, sadly yet redemptively, how real life is under the sun on this side of eternity. This is a book that you will carry in your heart for years to come. And it will remind you that in this life we can live with certainty about the life to come. I encourage you to cuddle up in a cozy place, let go of your preoccupations and enter into the pathos of this real-life journey. It will deliver you to a place of greater understanding and heart renewal about what's really important in life, and how we are to live it. I have known Grace Walker for many years, and more recently watched her fight for her life as a few years ago, on a snowy day, she and her husband were in a head on collision which took his life. Making an arduous but slow recovery, she began to reflect upon her life looking at it through a different lens; and now you will hold her heart in your hands. This is powerful and good stuff. Read it thoroughly. You'll be glad you did.

Rev. Dr. R. Edgar Bonniwell

We have been speaking with Grace Walker, author of *Now I Can Think Myself to Mars*. It is a touching book filled with a sincere faith and a relationship with God and Jesus and a walk with mother and son who were able to communicate so beautifully.

Grace Walker and her family are people of faith. On a travel trip, she and her son had a very meaningful conversation, especially for a child under 10. Within a short time, Nathan was gone, and their conversation reverberated within her, inviting her to share the insights gained.

Susan Sherayko
Rebuilding Your Life Radio
January 8, 2022 Episode

A Collection of
Poems and Prose
In Memory of My Beloved Son
Nathan Oliver Walker
1983-1992

Sketch by Shannan Hope Janney (nee Walker)

I go to prepare a place for you…
I will come back and take you to be with me
that you also may be where I am.
You know the way to the place I am going.

John 14:3b–4 NIV

Table of Contents

Professional Reviews v
About the Author xix
Acknowledgements xxi
Introduction xxiii
Prologue xxix
    The Final Gift xxxi
    The Master Gardener xxxv
    Enduring Peace xxxvii

Part I – Now I Can Think Myself to Mars 1

1992 - A Son's final Goodbye 3
    Mom, Remember When, Now I Can
    Mom's Letters of Response

1992 – 1997 – A Mother's Journal of Renewal 61
    A Mother's Discussion 63
    Living the Sentence 65
    A New Journey 67

1992-2008 – A Father's Heart 73
    A Second Strand 75
    Your Father's Heart 77
    The Silent Screamer 79
    A Trilogy - The Return of Laughter 81
        The Hard Comedy 83
        My Old Friend Laughter 85
        To the Giver of the Song 87

Creativity in Motion 89
I Hear Nathan 93
Road to Discovery 95
The Two Testimonies of Rick Walker 97
Three Strands 101

Part II – Observations Since Mars 103

2007-2013 Outgrowth of Renewal 105
   Outgrowth 107
   Playing God's Lottery 109
   They May Be Buzzards, But They Can Fly 117
   Hay Canyon 125
   Eighteen Years in Eternity Plus One 127
   Moving Right Along 129
   What Did You Go Out to the Desert to See? 131
   Imperfection 137
   Avoidance 141
   Beautiful on the Mountains Are Feet 145
   Assumptions 149

2013-2015 Concluding the Matter 153
   Vapors – An Incentive to Move Forward 155
   Going Home to the Mountains 161
   We're a Team 171
   A Walk of Grace 173

Epilogue 2015-2023 177
   Erbal Tease 179
   Incognito versus Assimilation 185
   Inspiration for "Lament of a Tarnished Vessel" 191
   Lament of a Tarnished Vessel 193
   Remember the Potter 197
   Survival in the Deserts of Life 201
   Inspiration for the Poem "Bedtime Prayer of a Warrior King" 209
   Bedtime Prayer Of a Warrior King 211
   Blessings and Comfort 215

Author Interviews 219

About the Author

The author published the first edition of *Now I Can Think Myself to Mars* in 2016 after retiring from a career as a nurse practitioner. Then fulfilling a long-held dream of attending Bible School, she earned a Master of Ministry from Ministry International Institute. She is now a licensed minister with Ministry International Inc.

Continuing to write of common occurrences as they relate to spiritual matters, Grace Hournbuckle Walker is developing a career as author and speaker. Her focus is encouraging others to seek relationship with God: Father, Son and Holy Spirit, to receive comfort, solace and guidance from the One who loves them best. Her writings include biblical references that can be used for personal or small-group discussion.

The author is retired after a forty-year career in nursing, first as an RN for five years then a nurse practitioner for the next thirty-five years. She has a BSN from the University of New Mexico in Albuquerque, and an MSN, FNP – Family Nurse Practitioner from the Medical College of Georgia in Augusta. She then received a Post Graduate Certificate, FPMHNP – Family Psychiatric &

Mental Health Nurse Practitioner from the University of Cincinnati in Ohio. During her last twelve years of practice, she specialized in Post-Traumatic Stress Disorder – PTSD. Concurrently, the author served on the faculty of the College of Nursing, University of Cincinnati in both family and psychiatric nurse practitioner programs during her last twenty years of practice.

After retirement, the author relocated to her home state of New Mexico after having lived for thirty-five years in Cincinnati, Ohio, except for a brief sojourn in Mobile, Alabama. For her first two years in New Mexico, the author alternated between a house in the desert and a mountain cabin, depending on her desire for heat or cold, geographically adjusting the thermostat of her personal HVAC. She then settled into the family cabin in the mountains for a year, enjoying mild summers, white winters, and mostly clear blue skies. The author then moved back to Ohio to be close to her daughter Shannan and family as well as to focus on completing the writing of the first edition of this, Nathan's *Mars* book.

Acknowledgements

To my daughter and best of friends, Shannan Hope Janney, my love and joy in sharing the journey. I love your beautiful sketch of Nathan displayed on the dedication page of this, his *Mars* book.

Thank you, Cousin Nita Johnson, for relocating into our lives here in Cincinnati. With your gift of photography, you provided a wonderful pictorial of Nathan's last year here.

Friends who shared Nathan's life here on earth, including neighborhood buddies, school friends, teachers, baseball teammates, and coaches, thank you for making his short time with us a rich experience.

My Ladies Group is a gathering of friends who have provided much-needed support as prayer partners and sounding boards while I have tackled this project of sharing Nathan's conversational gift and the Dear Nathan letters. Special thanks to Bonnie Sales, Cynthia Thompson, Ruth Foster, Sally Covert, and Tina Swinson for your prayers and encouragement as I worked on not only this current edition, but also the first edition in 2016.

Notable acknowledgement goes to Shirley Jackson, my girls' club leader in New Mexico who encouraged me when I was twelve years old to take responsibility for my thought life. I learned to "take every thought captive"[1] and to choose to "think about these things"[2]. Fifty years later after I moved back to New Mexico, Shirley once again provided prayerful support while encouraging me to publish the first edition of Nathan's poem and my devotional writings.

In heartfelt gratitude for graciously reviewing the first edition of the manuscript for scriptural integrity, I express my thanks to the Reverends Chester Hournbuckle, Justin Crispin, and Dr. R. Edgar Bonniwell. Thanks also goes to Rev. Chester Hournbuckle for reviewing the 2nd edition as well.

My warm appreciation to my editor at iUniverse in the 2016 publication, for rounding out my submitted chest of verbal quilt pieces into an heirloom design that supports my vision for this book: to share my son's anticipation of the ultimate adventure—traveling into eternity.

Thank you ReadersMagnet team for your patience and expertise throughout the process of republishing this book, which contain not only new chapters in my life, but also new insights while continuing my journey. Thank you for providing the book cover design for the 2nd edition.

---

1 2 Corinthians 10:5
2 Philippians 4:8-9

Introduction

Now I Can Think Myself to Mars is a phrase reminiscent of my final conversation with my eight-year-old son Nathan, in June 1992, while on a road trip. While traveling, he had excitedly discussed the possibilities that will be available to him after "I die and go to Heaven", including the ability to "travel like Jesus". The very next day Nathan died suddenly from what was later determined to be a twisted blood vessel in his abdomen. He'd been in the hospital a couple of times but would recover after a few days. We had not been given any reason to expect a life-threatening situation. This book is in memory of Nathan's life here below as well as his thoughts regarding the possibilities that would become available "when I get my new body like Jesus." Nathan's story, as well as our family's, are portrayed in Part I of this book which is also entitled *Now I Can Think Myself to Mars.*

The **Prologue** consists of three letters. The first two were written from me to Nathan for the 1st edition. Then I wrote the third letter for this 2nd edition. I was inspired to write the first letter in November 1992 the day before what would have been Nathan's ninth birthday here below. That morning, words of inspiration had been whispered to my heart, reflecting our last conversation which later grew into this, his *Mars* book, as I lovingly call it. The second letter written in 2014 expresses my feelings of inadequacy as I contemplated beginning the overwhelming endeavor of writing not only Nathan's story, but our family's as well. My third letter is to you, the readers of this 2nd edition, discussing the unwavering focus, which was crucial in leading me into grief, through survival and continuing on into flourishing.

Part I – Now I Can Think Myself to Mars on Nathan's story of not only his life here below, but also glimpses into the possibilities now available to him in his forever-after life. This section also deals with our loss of Nathan and the ways in which my family and I dealt with that loss and adjusted to life without him. This section covers not only our final conversation and events of his brief life, but also follows our family's continuing path forward. It is our story over the next five years comprised of three subsections entitled **A Son's Final Goodbye, A Mother's Journal of Renewal** and **A Father's Heart.**

> **A Son's Final Goodbye** is a poem birthed out of Nathan's and my conversation the day before his passing while on a road trip. Five months later, the day before Thanksgiving 1992, I awakened with Nathan's voice running through my mind. Words mirroring Nathan's thoughts and musings on our final day together echoed within my soul. In this poem, aspects of our final conversation as well as brief events of his life are summarized. Each summary begins with "Mom, Remember

When..." A counterpoint then follows each summary "Now...". These counterpoints are descriptions of what I imagine Nathan's new reality in heaven to be. Following each of these are my letters to Nathan which reflect my thoughts and feelings for him regarding our conversation.

A Mother's Journal of Renewal is comprised of additional writings spanning the first five years after Nathan's passing. These journal entries focus on losing him and the ways in which my family dealt with such a loss. Also discussed is how we began adjusting to the "new normal" of life after Nathan's passing. Each in our own way had to allow ourselves to grieve and yet, as time passed, also live fully because that kind of acceptance is an integral part of what true faith is about. Together they show the path of this mother's grieving process and how that process helped me to continue walking out my journey of faith.

A Father's Heart is a compilation of the reflections and process of my husband Rick, Nathan's father. Included are some of his earlier writings which are applicable to any great loss not just of a child. This section also conveys Rick's impact on my own journey.

Part II – Observations Since Mars are some of my journal entries written over the following twenty-five years after those in Part I above. These inspirational letters are written to Nathan as if he lives on the other side of the world and I am just catching him up on things back home. This portion is divided into **Outgrowth of Renewal** and **Concluding the Matter.**

> **Outgrowth of Renewal** portrays me coming full circle, showing a mother's journey while reflecting thoughts and feelings regarding various situations and common occurrences of daily life. An example is an account of watching a group of buzzards floating in concert while catching a cool breeze over the top of the dam. I contemplate that although given what one might regard as a distressing mission or situation, buzzards are incredibly blessed by their creator with an *ability to rise above it all and FLY!*
>
> **Concluding the Matter** are my further musings on moving forward and my reassessment of previous conclusions I had made after Nathan passed away. It also reflects my thoughts at the time of publishing the first edition of this book versus my current views on the subject of death.

The **Epilogue** contains poems and essays written as I processed the possible results of spilling my guts to the world by having published such a personal story as my 2016 edition, of this, Nathan's *'Mars'* book. This section also reflects my current quest to identify Father God's purpose and assignments for me going forward as it relates to His Kingdom here on earth.

Prologue

1992-2023

The Final Gift

November 26, 1992
Cincinnati, Ohio

Dear Nathan,

I greatly miss you here on this side of eternity, but I am glad you get to enjoy your exciting new life in the forever hereafter. Remember our conversation the day before you left unexpectedly last June? We were traveling that weekend to visit Grandma and Grandpa near St. Louis. We traveled in bliss, unaware of the events that would transpire within the next twenty-four hours to propel you into eternity, leaving only memories behind: bittersweet memories of your oh-so-brief time with us and also memories of our last conversation.

Yesterday morning, the day before your first birthday away from us, your ninth birthday, I awoke with your voice running through my mind reflecting portions of our last conversation.

> *Mom, remember when I could travel so fast on my bike with the wind whistling through my hair?*
> *Now I can think myself to Mars.*

Words resonating with events of your brief live and our final conversation five months earlier, echoed within my soul. Your comments and questions that day form the basis for what I call your conversational poem, *A Son's Final Goodbye*. Father God had inspired your final gift to us: your musings about what your body will be like when you die and get a body like Jesus. You shared joyful hope and anticipation of a future in heaven. Within twenty-four hours, your expectation became your reality.

Your excitement of the possibilities of space travel "after I get my new body like Jesus", reverberated in my mind. And I thought, "I should write this down; maybe I can use it in a poem." Why I would consider writing a poem is a wonder because I haven't written a poem since fourth grade! Nathan, your father is our family poet. However, grabbing a tablet and a pen from my bedside stand, I lay in bed writing inspirations whispered to my heart. Inspirations of not only our last conversation, but other memories and events as well in celebration of the eight and a half years you were able to spend with us here in this earthly realm. It is also a memorial to your knowledge of where you were headed and a clear roadmap to anyone wanting to meet you there.

Nathan, you were feeling great the day before you left, no pain and plenty of energy. On our trip from Cincinnati to Saint Louis to visit my parents, I would periodically pull into a roadside rest stop so you and Shannan could get out of the car to run and play. Memories of that last day and our conversation reflect your love and excitement for the greatest adventure available in life – a forever future with

Jesus. Our conversation was your final goodbye, a son's final gift orchestrated by a very loving Father God.

Love, Mom

The Master Gardener

August 13, 2014
Cincinnati

Dear Nathan,

Honesty compels me to be brutal. I am not capable of completing the task set before me—the overwhelming task of writing our *Mars* book. I must be ruthless with the truth—my inadequacies, my truth. Sitting on the deck in the morning sun, I am driven to distraction by my failings. Then, like the gentle breeze caressing my face, comes entreaty. "Must I take the talents I have placed within you and give them to one who has been proven faithful with more?"

Pondering the implication of this thought, based on Jesus's parable of the talents[3], I gaze at the root-bound iris sharing my space in the sun. I wonder if perhaps we are in the same pot. From where I sit, I am able to observe the gardener's label, "Swingtown Bearded Iris", and have no doubt of the potential inherent in that plant. However, like me, does the iris focus only on the spring now long past and the brown blades once green with promise but now limp in ruin? Despite summer's heat and the drought-seared tips, can

---
3 Matthew 25:14-30

it see growth still flourishing and believe the gardener's promise? Can it hope for embedded purpose, worth, and future blossoms too beautiful to withhold?

Once shared, can it trust the design of the gardener? Or is it for the iris or even for me to decide who walks the garden, who observes in appreciation the glory of dew upon the face of the flowering of life? Is my task, like that of the iris, only to bloom where I am planted, utilizing the talents and experience at my disposal? Concluding this to be the case, I prepare to offer this collection of writings, and of necessity, commit the flourishing of this endeavor into the hands of the Master Gardener.

Love, Mom

Enduring Peace

August 2, 2023
Cincinnati, Ohio

Dear Reader,

My continuing journey reinforces the enduring connection to Nathan and to God, and the constant support, comfort, and inspiration that connection gives me. To survive it was and continues to be, crucial for me to focus on what God *did*, not on what he *did not* do. He did not heal Nathan's earthly body. What God *did*, was flood the scene with an overwhelming peace that passes all understanding as I watched the ending of my beloved son's earthly life and the beginning of Nathan's forever-healed life.

That sense of incredible peace accompanied my journey of grief and on into the renewal awaiting. Walking on, always in faith, I learned not only courage and acceptance, but also humility and surrender. For these comprise the essence of faith, hope and love. This was God's gift to me, a continuing gift for the rest of my journey. Now thirty-one years later I continue to discover nuggets of spiritual truth in common situations and observations in life. I also continue to experience God's gift of peace while discovering more of my Creator as well as more about not only myself, but also my spiritual walk.

I pray you experience peace in who the Lord God, our Creator is and who you are in him. May you always walk in our Lord's presence.

Grace Hournbuckle Walker

Part I

◆

1992-2008

Now I Can Think Myself to Mars

1992
A Son's Final Goodbye

A Son's Final Goodbye is a poem highlighting portions of Nathan's last conversation and events of the eight and a half years here below. Each stanza begins with "Mom, Remember When..." and a counterpoint then follows "Now...". These counterpoints are descriptions of what I imagine Nathan's new reality in heaven to be. Following each of these are my letters to Nathan which reflect my thoughts and feelings for him regarding that particular topic of his conversations or experiences.

Mom, Remember When...

In the emergency room in Saint Louis, you were
watching the doctors and nurses working on me

Then, knowing I wasn't coming back
you turned away, toward the wall

And saw me standing by Jesus
Who said to you, "It's okay"

Now...

I'm living with Jesus!

Love, Nathan

Dear Nathan,

As I was growing up, I remember hearing my mother on many occasions speak of three near-death experiences during her struggles with asthma. As I recall the story, during one near-death adventure your grandma rose out of her body. From the ceiling of the hospital emergency room, she looked down at the doctors and nurses trying to revive her. She also saw your grandpa standing over to the side in the room. Then she was met by her brother, Herbert who had died a couple of years earlier. He traveled with her to heaven, where she saw Jesus standing on the other side of a river.

My mom "knew" that if Jesus stretched his hands out toward her, she would stay in heaven, but if not, she would return. She was willing to stay, as urged by her brother, but was reluctant to leave her husband and children alone. However, Mom said that as she watched, Jesus's hands remained at his side. She then swiveled slowly around and immediately was back in her body! Instead of a near-death experience, I would call this a near-life experience, since in heaven we will be more alive than we are here!

Your Uncle Chester remembers Mom telling him additional details to the same near-death experience. When your Grandma returned to her body, your Grandpa was sitting beside her, holding her hand. She heard the doctors telling him that they were signing the death certificate. But my mom was unable to let them know she was back.

Then Daddy felt her squeeze his hand and he told the doctors, who said it was just a spasm which can happen after death. When he felt her squeeze his hand again, he told the doctors who responded, "Mr. Hournbuckle, your wife is dead!" Asking God to help her let the doctors know she was back ... one word was then heard. "Perry." - My dad's name coming from my mother's lips!

Nathan, on the day in June 1992 when you were in the emergency room, I refused to leave because I wanted you to "see" that I stood close by even at the end! I sat on top of a table just inside the door as the medical team frantically tried to change the course of time. After a while, knowing that you weren't coming back, I turned away to stare straight ahead at the wall. Then I saw Jesus—and you, Nathan. You were standing a little behind him and to his left, peaking around Jesus like a child hiding behind a parent when confronted by new and unexpected events.

You and Jesus glowed so bright, and it was a glow so white that there are no earthly words or examples to compare! I could not see your features due to the brilliance of the light coming from you, but I could tell that you both were wearing robes. Then Jesus, looking straight at me, said "It's ok." Up until last year, in 2022, while relating this experience, I never mentioned to anyone that I saw Jesus's face clearly when he made eye contact while speaking to me. The clarity of his face was as clear as his words. And Jesus calmed the storm within my spirit, such peace enveloped me, and I knew it really was okay! It's unexplainable how any of this could possibly be "Ok" but the peace of God made it so.

Remember in the Bible when Jesus took Peter, James, and John up the mountain? Scripture states that his appearance was changed: "His face shone like the sun, and his clothes became as white as the light"[4]. This describes how you and Jesus looked that day in the emergency room.

Nathan, you left your earthly body for a far better one, a body like Jesus's. After the struggle to keep you here was lost, the nurses allowed me to help them. As I washed your face and placed a gown on your now still form, I repeated to the nurses all that you and I had talked about the day before. Your conversation about what heaven would be like, what kind of body you would have, and the things you would be able to do when you went to be with Jesus. What an adventure I know you are having now with your Jesus!

Love, Mom

---

4 Matthew 17:1-3 NIV

Mom, Remember When...

We went to Lunken Airport for
what was to be our last Easter together

We walked the five-mile path
and played on the playground's planes and trains

It was so peaceful that day
and you took lots of pictures

Now...

Because of how Jesus spent the first
Easter here on earth

I get to live in heaven with him
and enjoy his great gift of peace

                    Love, Nathan

Dear Nathan,

Your name, Nathan Oliver Walker, means "one who walks in God's gift of peace". Well, really Nathaniel would be "God's gift"; however, we know that you were indeed a gift from God to us, even for the short time that you were here. And like your name, you also walked in God's peace as well. However, sometimes I would have to remind you that "Oliver" means "peace". But mostly your "fighting" was in play.

I remember one day when you came into the kitchen after playing outside with your friends. You were concerned that you wouldn't be able to fight in heaven. "And you do know how much I like to fight!" you said with that special smile of yours. I assured you that if you couldn't fight in heaven, God would find something for you to do that you would enjoy just as much!

Shannan was just six years old, and you were eight when you left. Remember how you used to wrestle with your little sister every day and let her pin you to the floor? You would struggle with much grunting, groaning and grimacing. After you were gone, I made an effort to wrestle with Shannan at some point each day. I knew she missed her big brother greatly. One day, as we wrestled on the floor and she was pinning me down as I struggled, she said, "Mommy, wrestling is a kind of hugging, isn't it? That's the kind of hugging Nathan and I would do, huh?"

You loved your little sister so much! You also loved Nicole, your big sister. She turned sixteen the month after you left. Because she was your half-sister, after the age of fourteen, she left our household off and on, for visits or having gone to live with her mother for six months. However, during the last few months of your time here, she was home with us.

Nathan, you continue to walk out your life of peace in heaven, and indeed you were also a gift of peace to us during the time you spent here. With you gone, God has given us the gift of peace "that passeth all understanding"[5] to ease our loneliness. We will see you again someday soon, Nathan. Until then, please give Jesus a big "hug" for us.

Love, Mom and Shannan

---

[5] Philippians 4:7 KJV

Mom, Remember When…

I said that babies who die are lucky
because they get to be with Jesus

But they're unlucky
because they don't get to have a life here

Now...

I'm lucky because
I get to be with Jesus, and

I'm not unlucky because
I had a life on earth too!

Love, Nathan

Dear Nathan,

You are one of those individuals who know how to fully enjoy the moments of your life: baseball, family, friends, playing, creek walking, swimming, swinging, biking, and hiking at the lake. There was so much exuberance in the things you did. I remember looking out the kitchen window one blustery winter day. There, you and your dad were leaning back into the wind at almost a forty-five-degree angle. Then you just let yourself go and were "blown" across the yard!

There are people content to watch the excitement, but you were compelled to experience the moments presented to you. This was indeed a great gift. The Word teaches us to live life today trusting in Father God, because we do not know what tomorrow holds and each day has its own trouble[6]. Even with uncertainties especially after hospitalizations, you still enjoyed your todays! I am so glad that you were also able to enjoy the promise of the Father to take care of your tomorrows. I know you are having fun in your great hereafter.

Love, Mom

---

[6] Matthew 6:33–34

Mom, Remember When...

I asked, "If babies don't know Jesus, how do they get to heaven?"

"Babies and anyone whose minds haven't grown up enough to know right from wrong go to heaven"

With a crooked grin and a sideways glance,
I said, "I don't know right from wrong"

You just grunted, "Uh-huh"

Then softly,
"But, Mom, I have Jesus in my heart!"

Now...

Jesus has me in his arms!

Love, Nathan

Dear Nathan,

The Word says, "If anyone, then, knows the good they ought to do and doesn't do it, it is sin to them"[7]. It also says that all of us must come to him as a child[8] with childlike faith that freely accepts forgiveness. "For with the heart one believes unto righteousness, and with the mouth confession is made unto salvation"[9]. And that each of us will stand before the judgement seat of Christ and give account of himself to God[10]. Scripture compares us to sheep, lost and unsure, depending on the shepherd. I need to be a lamb willing to be rescued from the cliff and cradled in the arms of the Shepherd. I need to be willing to let the Shepherd take me with him to a place of safety.

Unlike a little child, I, as an adult, try to reason with the Shepherd. "I'm not doing so bad leaning into this scrubby bush halfway down the cliff; the bush will hold, surely it will. Maybe I'm not on top of the mountain, but at least I haven't fallen as far as those other lambs down there. Look, Jesus, why don't you leave me alone. I don't need your help. I may be a lamb, but I can grip the craggy places with my hoofs and pull myself up and over the top."

---

[7] James 4:17 NIV
[8] Matthew 18:3
[9] Romans 10:10 NKJV
[10] 2 Corinthians 5:10

Or if knowing I can't do it myself, I bargain, "Okay, Jesus, you lift me up. I will trust you for that, but then I will tell you where to take me, what to prepare for me, who to bring into my life, and what I need next." Can you imagine a lost sheep talking to its shepherd like that? Especially after being rescued? I tend to want total control even when I have never been to the place where I now find myself! But Jesus, the Shepherd, can see over the cliff and has been to all my times and places, and is experienced in caring for the lost little lambs of his flock.

Nathan, I know you are safe in his arms, and I also know that he can care for us here while we wait for the right time to see you again.

Love, Mom

Mom, Remember When…

During last spring's beginner swimming
how I was a little bit

Afraid to jump off the diving board
but by my second turn, I did a flip

Now…

I swim in the River of Life!

Love, Nathan

Dear Nathan,

When you were on that diving board for the first time, you looked hesitant, but when you got back into line for the second time, it was a different story. Although you had taken swimming lessons at the lake, that day at the pool was the first time you had ever been in water over your head. But, readying yourself for adventure, you took your place again on the diving board! You did a flip off the board, my heart skipped, and your swimming teacher yelled, "No more flips, just jump!"

Even as a very little guy, you were adventurous. Once in our driveway, you crawled around while I pulled weeds nearby. A neighbor's lawn mower started up, and you immediately looked up and started crawling toward the sound. You weren't frightened, just intrigued by the sound of power revving to life. Were you curious about the source?

By the time you were four years old, you and your buddy from next door were ramping bikes. Scavenging through both of your yards and carports, you would come up with some interesting ramps. Having been uniquely designed and constructed by preschoolers, the ramps frequently didn't survive your demolition rides. That's where my skills with cleaning up scrapes and applying band aides came in handy. Someone might ask, weren't the training wheels a problem? Didn't they get in the way? However, the only training wheels you had, were the running rhythm of your father's feet as he steadied you or ran beside you while you learned to balance. And then you were off, constantly exploring ways to make riding more exciting, thus the ramps.

Although hesitant at first, with Jesus in the emergency room, I'm confident that you were drawn to the ultimate adventure. Did you not only hear the power but also see Jesus and were drawn to the source ramping you up into the ultimate life? What was your trip to heaven like? We once took my mom to a surround theater that had a short introductory segment where we traveled through space at warp speed with stars streaking past! Remembering your grandma's description of one of her near-life experiences, I leaned over to whisper in her ear. "Mom, is that what it's like to travel to heaven?" Her response was with a voice of remembered wonder: "This is exactly what it's like!"

Love, Mom

Mom, Remember When...

You took me ice-skating
last winter for the first time

I had never even been on roller skates
except on the carpet at home

I was ice-skating on Fountain Square
while it snowed and

doing wobbly twirls without falling down
...well, sometimes

Now...

You should see me!

Love, Nathan

Dear Nathan,

Because we didn't live in a neighborhood with sidewalks, remember how I used to let you and Shannan practice roller-skating in the house on the carpet? I wanted you to be able to learn control without it being too slippery. You were both getting pretty good, and we were planning the next step to a skating rink. However, we ended up on a family outing downtown at Fountain Square on a snowy winter day and actually ice-skated! I must admit that although I learned to roller-skate as a child, I had never ice skated before either.

Not planning for the ice rink, I had not brought any gloves. Shannan's little hands were getting so red from catching herself with her hands on the ice. A kind lady took pity on her and lent her a pair of the one-size-fits all gloves. With the immediate need of Shannan's hands taken care of, I turned my attention to you with a mother's caution, urging you not to try twirls until you learned to ice-skate. However, you were never one to put off an exciting experience. Nathan, the look on your face as you skated around practicing twirls was a joy to my heart!

Beautiful as each of the seasons are, why won't we still be able to enjoy the changing splendor? The Bible describes the river of life in the New Jerusalem coming down from heaven as "...shining like crystal and was flowing from the throne of God and of the Lamb down the middle of the street of the city. The tree of life grows on each side of the river. And it produces fruit twelve times a year, once each month. The leaves of the tree are for the healing of all the nations"[11]. Could this perhaps be describing the seasons and the river of life when it is frozen over for ice-skating? After all, not all of us are from the tropics, and therefore, some of us do enjoy the fun aspects of winter as well as the other seasons! Right now, you could be ice-skating in heaven on a crystal river. But I guess you don't need me to tell you to be careful anymore, do you? Have fun.

Love, Mom

---

11 Revelation 22:1-2 NCV

Mom, Remember When...

I could travel so fast on my bike
with the wind whistling through my hair

Now...

I can Think Myself to Mars!

Love, Nathan

Dear Nathan,

As we traveled to Saint Louis, our conversation centered on what your life would be like after you died and went to be with Jesus.

"Mom, when we get to heaven, the Bible says we will be like Jesus, so I'll have a body like Jesus, right? I'll be able to travel so fast. I bet Jesus travels *really* fast!" Pausing in thought, "No, he doesn't. He doesn't have to *travel* anywhere. He just *thinks* himself someplace! And I'll have a body like Jesus, so when I die and get my new body, *I can think myself to Mars!*" You were so joyful and excited, imagining the ultimate adventure.

I can think of examples of this type of travel in the Bible when someone was suddenly elsewhere. On the third day after Jesus was crucified, he walked along with two of his followers who were going home from Jerusalem and discussing the horrifying events in Jerusalem. Not recognizing Jesus, they asked him to stay for the evening meal. Jesus blessed the breaking of the bread and as he did, they recognized him. Jesus then disappeared from their presence and the two men immediately returned to Jerusalem. While the two were telling his disciples gathered in Jerusalem, of their experience, Jesus appeared in their midst[12]. They had been gathered behind locked doors, fearing for their own lives, when

---

[12] Luke 24:13-35

Jesus suddenly appeared in the room[13]. However, Jesus wasn't the only one to travel in this way. Phillip had a similar experience after teaching the eunuch on the road from Jerusalem to Gaza. After baptizing the man, "the Spirit of the Lord suddenly took Phillip away, and the eunuch did not see him again, but went on his way rejoicing. Phillip, however, appeared at Azotus and traveled about preaching the gospel in all towns until he reached Caesarea"[14]. I think you might be right, Nathan. There's no need to travel fast when you can just *be there* by the Spirit.

I am glad that you are now able to enjoy God's creation unbound by earth's constraints. The Word says that Jesus was from the beginning and that "through him all things were made; without him, nothing has been made that was made"[15]. The living God "richly provides us with everything for our enjoyment"[16], which includes the earth, the stars, and the planets. I am glad that you are now able to enjoy all of God's wondrous creations in a much fuller way than ever before, and yes, perhaps even think yourself to Mars.

Love, Mom

---

[13] Luke 24:36 John 20:19
[14] Acts 8:39–40 NIV
[15] John 1:1–3 NIV
[16] 1 Timothy 6:17 NIV

Mom, Remember When…

The day before I came to heaven, I asked

"Was the boy who led Samson
to the two pillars a boy like me?"

"Yes"

"Did that boy die too?"

"Yes, honey, he did.
Everyone died

And Samson had a greater victory
in his death than any his whole life"

Now...

You wonder if I knew
I was going to die

Love, Nathan

Dear Nathan,

As we pulled away from the house to go on our trip, I wondered why you panicked. You didn't want to go without your dad, who had stayed to work, while we were to enjoy a week with Grandma and Grandpa near Saint Louis. I reassured you that everything would be okay, and you settled down. Another unusual thing about the trip was that you became fretful and fearful upon seeing a dead deer along the side of the road, apparently killed in traffic. In our part of the country, this was a common occurrence. I reassured you, "It's only a deer, Nathan. Why are you so upset?"

As we drove, we had been listening to a set of children's Bible story tapes that Grandma had given to you kids. After the story about Samson, you asked about the little boy. At the time, I thought you meant: did the little boy die with Samson? I had no inkling that events were to transpire the next day that would give new meaning to your question. "Was the boy who led Samson to the two pillars a boy like me? Did that boy die too?"

A couple of weeks after you were gone, the mother of one of your friends came over. She said her son had told her about a dream he'd had a few days before our trip to Saint Louis. "Mom, I dreamed Nathan died in a faraway place." I also found out that although you did not see this friend after the dream, another friend who was close to both of you repeated the dream to you. It would explain why you were so focused on heavenly things.

Love, Mom

Mom, Remember When…

I asked you if after I go to heaven and get my new body I could come back and see what is happening here

You answered "I don't know, honey, You'll have to wait and ask Jesus when you see him"

Sixteen hours later I was with him

Now...

I know the answer!

Love, Nathan

Dear Nathan,

I had no idea of the significance of our conversation as we drove to Saint Louis, but I will be forever grateful for your precious gift to us: your view of your forever life. If I had known then, how close the reality loomed on our horizon, could I have changed anything? Scripture tells us that when we are formed in our mothers' wombs, God already has written in his book the number of the days ordained for us[17]. I am indeed comforted that he has plans not just for our days here, but for that special day when we go home to be with him. A verse in Psalms says "Precious in the sight of the Lord is the death of his faithful servants"[18]. Sometimes those of us left behind are able to see the beginning of someone's journey into their next life, as I did when I saw you and Jesus standing in that emergency room. And sometimes we are given just a little peek into another's experience.

My Granny Johnson shared such a peek during Christmas time 1985 with two of her eight children, Uncle J, one of the oldest and Aunt Lena the youngest. I remember being told of Granny's conversation a few days before she passed away. "Where is your daddy?" My Uncle J answered, "Momma, Daddy has been gone several years. Did you see him? Did you talk to him?" She responded, "No, I

---

17 Psalm 139:13–18
18 Psalm 116:15 NIV

didn't talk to him, but he was just here standing at the foot of the bed." She went home to heaven a few days after that.

Near the time of Uncle J's own journey home many years later, my Aunt Lena had gone to visit her big brother. She had been there the day before, but on this particular day when his baby sister walked into the house, he said to her, "Bye, baby." She replied, "But I just got here. I'm not going anywhere." He then responded that Grandpa was telling him to come home. While visiting Aunt Lena in the summer of 2023, she clarified what Uncle J (short for WJ) had said. "Daddy is waving me home." And it is only as I review this letter for the 2nd edition of this *Mars* book that I realize the full significance of Grandpa "waving him home."

You will think it is as cool as I do once you understand. You see, when I was a kid, Uncle J, then in his thirty's, played baseball. I can still see him and his team in their striped uniforms. It was exciting to watch them play when we would be visiting the Texas branch of the family.

Many years later as Uncle J was swiftly rounding third base in his last game of the season of life and focusing on scoring his final run, he saw his daddy standing on the other side of the plate, "waving him home". Isn't that amazing? Uncle J's Home Run waved in by his daddy and celebrated by the crowd in the stands as well as the team owner, his son and the coach: Father God, Jesus the Son and Holy Spirit!

Sometimes we get a glimpse of our loved ones' new lives in other ways. My brother, Chester, was telling me not too long after you had gone that he had seen you in a dream. You know, one of those "real dreams" that are just as real as life? In the dream, he and his family were coming to visit us, and as they were driving up to the house, it was late at night. Everyone else in the car was asleep. He said that you were playing around that big old tree at the corner of the house by the front door. "Nathan, shouldn't you be in bed?" he asked. "I don't have to go to bed anymore," you replied. "Well, shouldn't you at least go inside and let your mother know you're here?" And you said, "No…it's not time yet! Tell my mom hello for me." Only God knows the meaning of dreams like these. The Prophet Jeremiah tells us that God has "… plans to prosper you and not to harm you, plans to give you hope and a future"[19].

You may have already met up with him and so already know, but one of our friends died that first year after you. Your father and I were told of the following unusual experience. This friend was driving down the road, alone in his truck, when suddenly he felt that he was no longer alone. Looking over to the passenger seat, there you sat! He said that you weren't ghostly in appearance but as real and solid as you ever were when you were still here! You didn't say a word but just smiled! He described it as a smile of peace. Then you were gone! Our friend said that this encounter gave him a sense of peace and comfort during his final illness, which was diagnosed shortly after he had seen you riding in his truck.

How precious is the sharing of these brief glimpses of our friends and loved ones' transitions into eternity. A son, a brother, a grandparent, uncle or friend – all these are just glimpses into the

---

19 Jeremiah 29:11 NIV

continuation of life into the eternal heavenly realm. In a letter to the believers in Corinth, Apostle Paul wrote that "We are confident, I say, and willing rather to be absent from the body and to be present with the Lord"[20].

He knew he could rely on Jesus's promise as written in the book of John…

> I go to prepare a place for you…
> I will come back and take you to be with me
> That you also may be where I am.
> You know the way to the place I am going[21].

Love, Mom

---

20 2 Corinthians 5:8 KJV
21 John 14:2b-4 NIV

Mom, Remember When...

We stood on the observation deck
on top of Carew Tower last winter while it snowed

We watched the ice-skaters
far below, on Fountain Square

Now…

I'm a part of the
"Great Cloud of Witnesses"

                    Love, Nathan

Dear Nathan,

I have always been intrigued by the scripture regarding the "great cloud of witnesses" [22]. Remember the crowd in the stands cheering as Uncle J scored his last home run in my last letter? They were the great cloud of witnesses! Apostle Paul wrote in Hebrews of many of the ancients who were commended for faith which he described as having "confidence in what we hope for and assurance about what we do not see" [23]. Many others were mentioned, not by name but by their deeds. Paul went on to say "since we are surrounded by such a great cloud of witnesses, let us throw off everything that hinders and the sin that so easily entangles. And let us run with perseverance the race marked out for us, fixing our eyes on Jesus the pioneer and perfecter of faith" [24].

I have had to do just that to survive your passing— fix my eyes on Jesus! I have had to look forward, not back to when you were here on earth with us. The Word teaches us not to look backward but to plow on with our faces to the future [25]. Someday I will again see you face-to-face, but until then, Nathan, until then I must of necessity be continually looking to Jesus!

Love, Mom

---

22 Hebrews 12:1
23 Hebrews 11:1 NIV
24 Hebrews 12:1-2a NIV
25 Luke 9:62

Mom, Remember When…

I was excited about
that feast we're going to have
when we all get to heaven

Can you imagine
what the food will taste like

We will be able to eat as much as we want!"

Grace Hournbuckle Walker

Now...

I watch the angels
getting it ready!

Love, Nathan

Dear Nathan,

You always did have a passion for food. Your first prayers at a very young age sounded like our weekly grocery list. "God, thank you for hot dogs and ice cream, thank you for bananas and hamburgers and chips and cookies and spaghetti and peanut butter and…" I remember coming into the kitchen when you were two and catching you with the pan of brownies. Nathan, you had a brownie in each hand and one in your mouth. When you saw me, your little hands stuffed the brownies into your mouth, and you were off! Running as fast as your legs could carry you out the back door and up the hill in the yard! I didn't chase you because I didn't want you to choke on the amount of brownies you had just stuffed into your mouth… Ahh, this life's limits.

Nathan, on our trip that last day, you surmised that we wouldn't have to stop eating because we were full, and we wouldn't have to go to the bathroom. "We can just keep eating for as long as we want!" During the last six months you were here with us, there were many times you couldn't eat because of abdominal pain and vomiting. So, I imagine that thinking of how different things would be in heaven and at the great celebration feast[26] was of great comfort to you.

Love, Mom

---

26 Revelation 19:7–9

Mom, Remember When...

On our trip we talked about
Jesus calling to the disciples

To leave their boats and follow him
and he would make them "fishers of men"

You explained what a "fisher of men" was
and I was silent for a while

Now...

You wonder if I told Jesus
I was willing to follow him

And asked him to
make me a fisher of men.

                Love, Nathan

Dear Nathan,

I remember that Grandma was visiting a couple of weeks before you left us. At dinner one night, it was your turn to offer the blessing, and you ended with "and God, please don't let me die". I was shocked that you would think just because you had been in and out of the hospital a couple of times, that it was life threatening. Did you know that you would be leaving us?

We had discussed the story of Jesus walking beside the Sea of Galilee, and seeing Simon Peter and his brother Andrew, who were fishermen, casting a net into the lake. Jesus said to them, "Follow Me, and I will make you become fishers of men"[27]. During our trip to Saint Louis that last day, were you praying when you became silent after discovering what a "fisher of men" meant?

Were you thinking about Jesus asking you to leave this boat of earthly life and follow him, and become a fisher of men? What would this have meant to you? Would you be a fisher of men by your conversation, letting others know about heaven and how to get there? Were you thinking about what the effect on others would be when you left us? Did you wonder about the friends who you would be leaving behind?

---

27 Mark 1:16–20 NKJV

I am reminded of King Solomon's admonition in the Bible of casting your bread on the waters and, after many days, finding it again. A commentary I read stated that this might refer to King Solomon's trading of grain by sea. Several verses follow that allude to not letting uncertainty be an excuse for not making progress or investments[28]. Could this serve as an admonition to me to no longer delay the publishing of your story, but to invest it into other people's lives? As I sit here, I picture you in a boat casting the book with your poem upon the "waters" of life, thus further enabling you to become a "fisher of men".

Love, Mom

---

[28] Ecclesiastes 11:1-6

Mom, Remember When…

You and I sat on the white swinging chair in our
yard. We discussed the upcoming trip

In a couple of days you, Shannan and
I were going to Saint Louis

"We're on the same team, Nathan, so
I have to be able to rely on you"

I answered, as I held your hand and
raised it in the air

"We're a team, Mom, we're a team!"

Now...

I've done my part with my conversation
You've got to do your part

Tell them I'm in heaven with Jesus!
Tell them how to get here!

                Love, Nathan

Dear Nathan,

While your dad and I were at work one day, you and Shannan were at home with a sitter. However, you decided to walk quite a ways down a country lane to your friend's house without permission. After I got home, we discussed the importance of teamwork and dependability, especially on our upcoming trip to Saint Louis. Thus, your comment: "We're a team, Mom, we're a team!"

At your funeral service, I spoke, telling everyone about our last conversation as we drove to Saint Louis. How you talked excitedly of heaven and your anticipation of that great day. You expressed such joy about someday being with your Jesus and being like him! Later your Uncle Chester commented, "Nathan preached his own funeral." I sit here now and think, "Wow, what a blessing!"

Nathan, as you so eloquently described in your conversation, we must "have Jesus in our hearts" to be prepared for eternal life. Jesus stands at the door and knocks. "...if anyone hears my voice and opens the door, I will come in and eat with that person, and they with me" [29]. He doesn't turn us away; we can be friends of Jesus forever!

You are now living life more fully than you ever could here below because now you are with Jesus and indeed have a resurrected body

---

29 Revelation 3:20 NIV

like him. Scripture of Luke says "and they can no longer die; for they are like the angels. They are God's children, since they are children of the resurrection" [30]. You are no longer bound by the constraints of this earth, yet we are a team, Nathan. Yes, we are a team! I will tell them where you are and how to get there too.

Love, Mom

---

[30] Luke 20:36 NIV

1992-1997
A Mother's Journal of Renewal

A Mother's Journal of Renewal was written during the five years following Nathan's passing. These journal entries focus on losing him and the ways in which my family dealt with such a loss. They also show the path of this mother's grieving process and how that process helped me to continue walking my journey of faith.

A Mother's Discussion

January 1, 1996
Cincinnati

Dear Nathan,

In 1992, after you were gone, I prayed, "How long, Lord, do I have to endure this pain of Nathan's leaving?" *Whispered within my heart*[31] was "five years." *I thought to myself,* "I guess I can make it that long." Thus began my focus on surviving the next five years after which I fully expected to be with you in eternity.

I wrote the following poem in my journal every December and June over the next three and a half years, as few as one stanza at a time. It depicts the struggle of yearning for heaven to once again see the missing loved one, as well as the conflicting desire to be with those still here below.

Today, New Year's Day 1996, I pondered the reality of what my leaving would mean for the rest of the family if indeed I am rescued from my pain and reunited with you. Then, remembering

---

[31] Studies I had previously read prior to Nathan's passing had shown the intensity of one's grief on a daily basis typically diminishes over three to five years.

that a week or so after you were gone, I had heard a still small voice *whispering to my spirit*[32]. "You are so willing to come be with Nathan; aren't you willing to stay and be a part of the plan I have for Shannan's life?" Remembering my agreement, I now have not only *peace to my spirit* from Jesus the moment you joined Him, Nathan, but now, *solace*[33] *to my soul*[34] *as well.*

Love, Mom

---

[32] Spirit – Wisdom, Communion, and Conscience. John Paul Jackson, *The Art of Hearing God*, Revised Sixth Edition 1997-2014, pp 118.
[33] Solace - A source of relief or consolation
[34] Soul – Mind, Will and Emotions, John Paul Jackson, *The Art of Hearing God*, Revised Sixth Edition 1997-2014, pp 118.

Living the Sentence

1992 – 1996

June 1992 – Dec 1994

My life since June 1992
I live in six-month increments

Chunks of time to live through…five years to survive
All I have to do is make it six months at a time

Now it is December… Christmas
Only four and a half more years

I love June; Cherry trees blossomed to bright cherries
Only four more years to go

December again, Christmas, another chunk
Of time lived through

June… Birds love our cherries
I don't pick them anymore

Christmas…two and a half years left to survive
Another holiday just passed

June 1995 – January 1996

I plan how to prepare for my going
How to better Rick and Shannan's lives

We… I…was able to let go of Pearl Street
Where we lived with Nathan

To Deer Ridge, a better place for them
Made into a loving home before I go

What about Shannan?
When the cherries are again bright red times two?

What is the plan? She prayed not to be left behind
Then a whisper to my heart

"Don't you remember that first couple of weeks you agreed
To be a part of My plan for Shannan's life?"

"Yes, Lord."
"Then stop counting!"

A New Journey

January 1, 1997
Cincinnati

Dear Nathan,

The belief that I would see you again in five years, as depicted in the poem "Living the Sentence", was a private strategy for me to cope with the pain and loss of your death. Instead of interpreting the "five years" *whispered in my heart* as the length of time during which the sharpness of the pain would diminish, *I thought* that I would then be able to escape to join you in eternity. Although in no way did I want to be separated from my family here below, I simply could not face the thought of this intense pain for the next thirty or forty years. Therefore, this five-year belief enabled me to focus on your current reality and our future reunion instead of the day of your death and the ensuing loss.

In hindsight I realize that what we think in secret still seeps out into the awareness of those close to us. I deeply regret my use of this coping strategy, and its impact on my family. Imagine a child who is also missing the loved one but knows that their parent is looking forward to leaving him or her here alone and going to heaven to be with the other loved one. I so wish that I had kept my focus firmly on our lives here below while also acknowledging your new eternal life in heaven.

During this last year, I have been able to refocus on living my own life. This began my new journey—not my Five-Year Survival Plan but a Rest-of-My-Life Plan, whatever that may entail. Some readers of your conversational poem, *A Son's Final Goodbye*, may have the false impression that it was easy, that those of us left here below were able to rise above the sorrow to an ideal realm of bliss. It may seem to some that we did not experience the pain as we lived our life of faith. That's a false impression, for we did struggle in this new life. We weren't somehow "Super Christians" speaking out positive confessions. As many know firsthand, to continue our earthly life here below after one's child has died is one of the most difficult journeys we can take. It is a journey of many tears— more tears than I thought a person could cry. But it wasn't taken alone, *whispering to my spirit, the Lord assured me* that he is willing to be that "friend who sticks closer than a brother"[35] no matter how long I have left to me here below.

On several occasions it was implied, and in a couple of instances, I was told straight out, "If only you had had more faith, Nathan would not have died!" I replied then and I continue to respond: "I have to have faith in my God, not faith in my faith!" Abraham and Sarah also had this kind of faith; they "considered him faithful who

---

35 Proverbs 18:24b NIV

had made the promise"[36]. I also consider Jesus faithful, and he has promised me that I will again see you, Nathan.

Jesus told Peter "Let not your heart be troubled; you believe in God, believe also in me. In my Father's house are many mansions; if it were not so, I would have told you. I go to prepare a place for you. And if I go and prepare a place for you, I will come again and receive you to Myself; that where I am, there you may be also. And where I go you know, and the way you know." Thomas said to Him, "Lord, we do not know where you are going, and how can we know the way?" Jesus said to him, "I am the way, the truth, and the life. No one comes to the Father except through Me"[37].

In the kitchen one day, I cried out to the Lord. "God, I can't do this. I can't go on without hope." At that moment Shannan, who was six years old at the time, burst through the back door from playing in the yard. God spoke to my heart, "I gave you Hope!" I replied, "Yes, you certainly did. You gave me Shannan Hope Walker, 'wise one who walks in hope.'" The Lord named her from the beginning. He looked from the past, to beyond my now, and further on into our tomorrows. Yes, he's the one who gave us Shannan, a beautiful person in her own right who is such a treasure to enjoy, and whom I love deeply.

One night not long after you were gone, Shannan was fearful of going to sleep because she thought she might die in her sleep. I reassured her that if she were to die before she awoke, she would indeed awaken and you, Nathan, would be there to go to heaven

---
36 Hebrews 11:11b NIV
37 John 14:1-6 NKJV

with her. "Do you know anyone who that has happened to?" I said, "Sure, one time when your grandma died, her brother, who had died a few years before, met her at the top of the hospital room and traveled with her to heaven. But Grandma came back. And just before my granny died, she saw my grandpa in the room and knew she would be seeing Jesus soon. She knew that my grandpa had come back to go with her to heaven." In relief, Shannan turned over and went peacefully to sleep.

Confronted with death at such an early age affected your little sister's view of other events. Responding to the death of a pet, Shannan said, "It's only a cat; you can always get another cat." And regarding the certainty of everyone's appointment with death, she said, "Mom, I hope I die before you do." Upon seeing my stricken face, she added, "Maybe we can die at the same time." She paused in thought before saying, "But then Daddy would be all alone." Then brightening with a smile, "Maybe we can all go together."

Paul wrote to the Thessalonians, "Brothers and sisters, we do not want you to be uninformed about those who sleep in death, so that you do not grieve like the rest of mankind, who have no hope. For we believe that Jesus died and rose again, and so we believe that God will bring with Jesus those who have fallen asleep in him. According to the Lord's word, we tell you that we who are still alive, who are left until the coming of the Lord, will certainly not precede those who have fallen asleep... we who are still alive and are left will be caught up together with them in the clouds" (could this be a reference to that great cloud of witnesses?) "to meet the

Lord in the air. And so, we will be with the Lord forever. Therefore encourage one another with these words"[38].

So, I am indeed encouraged for we may yet "all go together."

Love, Mom

---

[38] 1 Thessalonians 4:13–18 NIV

1992-2008
A Father's Heart

A Father's Heart is a compilation of the reflections and process of my husband Rick, Nathan's father. Some of his earlier writings, applicable to any great loss are not limited to that of a child, are included. This section also conveys the impact Rick had on my own journey.

A Second Strand

Rick was a great source of support and comfort throughout our process of losing Nathan, grieving that loss, and learning to move forward. Reading Rick's writings helped me understand and relate to his own process of renewal. While following our individual paths as well as walking together in faith, ultimately Rick and I drew closer to each other.

Many times Rick literally took me by the hand pulling me with him as he went about his plans for that day. On evenings or weekends, he encouraged me to walk the track around the high school football field while he jogged. Each time he caught up to where I walked, Rick paused to see how I was doing before forging on down the track. Shannan would play near the track, walk with me or sometimes spend the time at a friend's house.

Although my final conversation with Nathan has continued to be a source of support and comfort in dealing with losing him—aside from God and my faith in him—Rick provided a different dimension that helped me greatly as I walked in faith, step by step, on this new journey. Enabled by Father God, Rick was the second strand in the rope I clung to, lending strength to my own walk of loss and renewal.

Your Father's Heart

June 13, 1998
Cincinnati

Dear Nathan,

Your father wrote the following collection of poems between 1983 and 1988 and presented this collection to our family in 1988. He'd had mono followed by some devastating years of ill health and wrote these poems as he began to recover from the initial fog of despair. Although "The Silent Screamer" and "The Return of Laughter" were written several years before you left for heaven, these poems are as applicable to our lives now as then. They portray themes that are congruent with the new journey thrust suddenly upon us on that June day in 1992 when you began your own eternal journey without us.

Seven months after writing the "The Silent Screamer", your dad wrote a trilogy, "The Return to Laughter." He was beginning to see some glimmering light of health and happiness again, and you had not yet graduated to your new life. The trilogy of poems speak of joy returning to life after a dark period. The theme of these poems was and remains appropriate after your passing, for the time eventually came for us to leave our valley of despair. It was a hard-fought climb for us, yet with a joy and peace that doesn't make any sense given the circumstances. This God-given peace allowed us to acclimate to the new heights required along the journey still before us. While we continue our lives here on earth, the joy of the Lord was, is, and will continue to be our strength. "Return to Laughter" is preceded by your dad's introduction and dedication to our family.

Now I will let your dad's words speak for themselves.

Love, Mom

The Silent Screamer

Richard Thomas Walker
May 18, 1988

A thought process…is freely addressed
To the person with the patience to wait
You may dislike…what you hear expressed
Yet, the hurting soul is not seeking debate

In the social crowd…he does not belong
The life lights are brightly aglow
Isolation and depression linger too long
The melancholy…swings high and low

He smiles too often as he learns to pretend
To project a self-image for everyone there
The silent screamer is desperate for a friend
To aid his recovery…from all the despair

No concern arrives…to where he stands
Sending messages that are never received
They must imagine…his life is so grand
When it is too bizarre…to be believed

If talking were the only therapy one needed
Then speak…to the caring ear…of course
Possibly all the pains that have proceeded
May be used…as a potential resource

Patterns of behavior are difficult to break
When a proper balance is drawn apart
The Lord Jesus I found truly will not forsake
The lonely cry…heard from the heart

A Trilogy—

The Return of Laughter

Hard Comedy
My Old Friend
To the Giver of the Song

Dedication:

To my wife Grace and children
Nicole, Nathan & Shannan
A statement of new hope
Merry Christmas 1988

-Richard Thomas Walker

The Hard Comedy

Richard Thomas Walker
December 1, 1988

You may have criticized the script before
It's a force of habit if you've seen it run
Showing in every neighborhood door-to-door
You'd know it…and just be glad it's done

My immunity to the theme is easy to believe
The hard comedy has finally been made a play
Stress and troubles that never want to leave
Title: "Welcome to Disaster, Enjoy Your Stay"

Everything takes money…everywhere you look
What is the finder's fee when I lose my head?
$9.95 he said…just to find the Blue Book
Nothing left but to use credit cards instead

I wonder who pays for it all…sure is nice
If just to sit back and not let myself worry
Put the drinks on my tab…and bring some ice
My perception of it all may be a bit blurry

Hindsight views misfortune as it fades away
The character denies the reality of defeat
Laughter volunteers to end the act each day
But is reluctant to call the play complete

The script you read is the only one found
Its words are translated on your life's stage
Grin and bear it, they say, as it comes around
Thank God the story ends…on another page

My Old Friend Laughter

Richard Thomas Walker
December 10, 1988

Well, it's about time, I had almost lost hope
No one used to explain what it was you meant
In your absence… I lacked the ability to cope
Laughter, you were always a spontaneous event

You are life's hero…of the hard comedy play
What happens…when one gets so out of touch
I trust your return brings a message to convey
Remind me now of the things I enjoyed so much

My friend… I recall as every day got its start
I would wake up laughing with new anticipation
I was a stand-up comic loving to share his heart
And contribute to life's great big celebration

Yes, there were days that now seem like dreams
A youthful enthusiasm and an amazing connection
An endless floating source of humorous themes
Were so kindly available for my daily selection

That certain gift…seems misplaced, my friend
Though my spirit and yours attempt to reconcile
I promise to remain open to what you recommend
Now that you're back, help me regain that style

To the Giver of the Song

Richard Thomas Walker
December 20, 1988

The sovereign source simply watched me drift
Across the desert… I have since left behind
I sing from the hymnal of cherishing the gift
The song of laughter…fills my spiritual mind

I laugh again…thank You, O Merciful Lord
That certain gift helps me regain that style
The inner joy… I have been unable to afford
Has miraculously awakened the emerging smile

My slaphappy mood is working around more now
And finally establishing habits of endurance
The old hard thoughts are chased away somehow
My new song has a theme…of solid assurance

To the Writer of the lyrics that my voice meets
Lord, You have been the Force of Love all along
With a cheerful spirit I shout to the streets
I do respectfully and willingly submit my song

Creativity in Motion

January 1, 2002
Cincinnati

Dear Nathan,

Your father is extremely creative. That creativity seems to take a different direction with each decade that passes; drawing in the seventies, writing poems and doing home upgrades in the eighties and nineties, and building barns, garages, and a cabin now in the singles. (I am still puzzled about what to call the first or even the second decade of the new millennium.) Throughout all these years, your dad continues to be a comedian with a type of humor that hits a person out of the blue with its spontaneity and creativity. Shannan takes after him in that way.

I have been focused on writing for several years now, yet while it takes me up to a week or two just to compose one page, your father completes writings or drawings within minutes or a few hours. When complimented on his sketches, he always responds, "All you have to do is put what you see on paper." In his younger years, he had attended the Art Academy for a short time, however, being limited to specific topics and styles for assignments, held no interest. Your father began writing poems during a phase of letter writing when, suddenly, everything he put to paper would come out in rhyme. He just could *not* write any other way.

When he began building projects around the house, not having learned the skills as a youth, he would check books out of the library to study. As he would work his way through a project, he would consult with more experienced men. However, due to his battle with chronic fatigue following mono in the early eighties, he frequently spends days with only enough energy to lie on the couch. How he envies men who have the strength and energy to be workaholics. He does acknowledge, however, that even with the health to work nonstop, it is not ideal to exclude other important aspects of life, such as God, family, friends, church and the community.

Although it is an earlier poem, I have included "I Hear Nathan," which your dad wrote when you were only eight weeks old, and he babysat you for the first time. I needed some "mom alone" time to go to the grocery store. Meanwhile, your father was trying to get in some "dad alone" time in front of his typewriter. However, Nathan, you insisted on your father's attention first and foremost. As depicted in this poem, your dad took time out to go upstairs, bring you into his space, and see to your wants as well as your needs.

Whenever I read about how your dad felt when you were a baby, I feel as if a film of your entire time with us here on earth is replaying in my mind's eye. At once you are an infant, a toddler, a small boy, and then a precocious eight-year-old. Your laughter, smile, and love fill my heart and my entire being, and the words of our last conversation before you journeyed to heaven fill me with peace.

These memories sustain me, but my unequivocal faith sustains me even more, for I know that I will be reunited with you in eternity through our shared love for Jesus. Until then, I can watch this movie again and again without end. Enjoy the poem—and enjoy watching the movie with me too.

Love, Mom

I Hear Nathan

Richard Thomas Walker
January 28, 1984

I can hear him now…over the intercom
Grunting, he's calling for someone to come
Louder, more fierce…now he is awake
How much more…can I take?

I better go get him…he's getting so mad
I'm sure I'd yell too…were I the little lad
Imagine just how he must feel…left all alone
And so new to this world…but what a tone

Here I come, son… I'll not leave you cry long
I love you; I'll help you, I'll even sing you a song
You're hungry, okay, but your mama's not here
Now take some of this formula, my little dear

It's not that? Oh, your diaper…could be a mess
I've changed them before, long ago, I must confess
Be patient, I'll check…it appears to be clean
You are a good boy…the best I've ever seen

Now downstairs we go…to see what there is to do
I was busy…let's see, how about a swing for you
Quite an invention…and you become so content
Now where was I, writing, yes, what words I have sent

I hear you, Nathan, but what…is there no time for me?
Saturday seems my only day… I expected to be free
Here I am…maybe if I crank this swing once more
Then I could get back to what I was doing before

You win, son… I can't argue with that
Now, now… Daddy's here, okay, try my hat
No? What is it then, son…that you demand?
Is it simply that your food not be so bland?

I hear you, Nathan…settle down, won't you try?
We will spend the day together, really, don't cry
I know, there, now, yes, you're no different from me
You want me to listen, give you love, before the plea

Road to Discovery

Dear Nathan,

Your father wrote the following testimony for our church's "getting to know you" project, although he is already well known because of his participation in the thespian ministry over the years. I guess his talent for this decade is acting. People at the church call him their Jimmy Stewart. But here is his story of how he became more involved in spiritual things and the Christian community.

The Two Testimonies of Rick Walker

Fall 2008

I grew up in a Catholic family of nine kids. I had a mostly happy childhood, but for a few struggles. As a teen I faded away from any good focus into endless fun in sports and then drinking at age fifteen. I thought I wasn't harming anyone, but in hindsight I may have hindered further achievement in life.

I got out of the army in 1971 and partied more until I got tired of it. I wanted something more, and while on a trip across the country in 1973, I was being prepared for what I was about to hear at a tent revival in Las Vegas. Every word spoken was exactly what I needed to hear, and I went forward to receive Jesus in my heart. I spent the next five years wondering what to do with this newfound faith, and I finally began to attend a full gospel church in 1978. Later I was baptized in water and have been going to church for thirty years now. However, having faith did not guarantee a life free from struggles. Many came—sickness and the loss of loved ones, the most difficult being the loss of my son, Nathan.

The miracle for me—my second testimony—is that God has given me the strength to go through it all without blaming him in anger and bitterness. Hardship can bring escape into drugs, alcohol, and suicide, but God protected me from all that.

The theme for all this was captured well for me in a song from the seventies: "On the Road to Find Out" by Cat Stevens. I had left home in Cincinnati determined to be clear of mind as I traveled out west, wanting to be open to any revelation of true life. That summer of 1973, at a tent revival in Las Vegas, God kicked out my sin and put me on a road to discovering life according to his Good Book, the Bible.

-Richard T. Walker

Dear Nathan,

Your dad's words from over the years, which I've shared with you here, come with his love and mine. Of course, you already know that.

Love, Mom

Note to reader – July 2023

Notice Rick's reference to the tent meeting in Las Vegas, Nevada 1973. Does the recent movie *Jesus Revolution* this Spring 2023 ring a bell? Until preparing this final manuscript for the second edition of this *Mars* book, I never thought about why Rick had headed out to California with some buddies. He had a personal determination to remain clear-minded and sober, describing it as going "on the road to find out". I was in high school and college during the late sixties and early seventies and that was to me just a common mindset of the times. Now I can see that it was God connecting with our generation in the throes of early adulthood. I am forever blessed that God intervened in Rick's life as he did fifty years ago. And God's doing it again. Now in 2023, he's connecting and reconnecting with today's generations.

Three Strands

Dear Reader,

I will close *A Father's Heart* in the same way that I opened it, emphasizing the deep positive impact Rick's sentiments had on me. Although we must each find and cultivate faith alone—as that walk is primarily a journey of solitude, except for God's eternal presence—knowing that we have a companion to share our experiences makes a huge difference. Rick was that necessary companion on earth for me, helping me refocus, accept our new life and achieve renewal as part of my journey of faith. Without him, I wonder how I would have survived after Nathan's passing. Walking not only in his own strength, Rick carried additional strength for me, that I needed but did not possess. With the strength of two entwined together as husband and wife, he embodied his name, Richard Thomas Walker, as "One who walks and leads with the strength of twins".

As the Good Book says, "Two are better than one, because they have a good return for their labor: If either of them falls down, one can help the other up. But pity anyone who falls and has no one to help them up. Also, if two lie down together, they will keep warm. But how can one keep warm alone? Though one may be overpowered, two can defend themselves. A cord of three strands is not quickly broken" [39]. As life rocked our world, we needed the strength the Lord brought as the third strand.

When Rick passed, our bond helped me do it all over again: to refocus and achieve acceptance and renewal, all as part of my journey of faith. It is for this very reason that I've shared his writings in this volume, placing them between my earlier and latter journey. Sooner or later, to survive with strength, we all have to take that walk of faith. Although this is a personal walk, recognizing our companions along the way helps us to acknowledge the constant, everlasting companionship of God. This third strand continues to be the strongest bond strengthening even to this day my own individual strand.

May you, the reader, avail yourself of the strength that our God offers in a very personal walk with Him through your own life. I pray that you do.

---

39 Ecclesiastes 4:9–12 NIV

Part II

2007-2015
Observations Since Mars

2007- 2013
Outgrowth of Renewal

Outgrowth of Renewal portrays me coming full circle, showing a mother's journey while reflecting thoughts and feelings regarding various situations and common occurrences of daily life. These inspirational essays are written to Nathan as if he lives on the other side of the world and I am just catching him up on things back home.

Outgrowth

Outgrowth of renewal is defined as a natural development resulting in movement toward or in the process of making something new or fresh again. Simply stated it means adjusting to our current situation to create healthy new beginnings. By so doing, this allowed me to refocus, which is the natural development toward making our lives new and fresh. It wasn't immediate, but a process over time. New and fresh is critical. It doesn't mean forgetting Nathan or not missing him. It is just living this new phase of life realistically. Rick was with me here on earth for part of it, but for much of it, he was my companion in outlook and perspective only. Nathan has been my companion in conviction and sentiment since his passing.

During this period, I continued to travel the path of loss, acceptance, and renewal. After Rick's passing, the only difference was that I was now coming full circle for a second time. Each time I reflected on Nathan and our final conversation, I would think of it in different terms because, although I had now lost Rick as well, he had been reunited with Nathan. And I, having survived one terrible loss, knew I could and would survive another.

I have learned to refocus, and that grants me the blessing of renewal. To put this another way, I have rounded out my walk of faith—or God has rounded it out for me, traveling from loss to acceptance and then through both of them a second time. It was that second revolution of the circle that brings me to stronger renewal, and to the peace, serenity, and wisdom that it brings. After all, that is what faith truly is.

Playing God's Lottery

August 25, 2007
Cincinnati

Dear Nathan,

I was thinking the other day what it would be like to play the lottery God's way. I have a Mega Millions lottery ticket in my purse, or pocketbook as my granny would have said. I bought it while helping Shannan drive back to college. Can you believe she is so grown up now?

I do not normally play the lottery, believing I have just as much of a chance of winning without buying a ticket. However, this is tradition: buying lottery tickets on our twice-a-year trek back and forth between Ohio and Florida. We used to buy one in each state, but as time passed, we tended to forget some states.

This time, her senior year, we played scratch-off in Tennessee and won eight dollars on our one-dollar ticket, and then played another two-dollar scratch-off and won two dollars. This, we promptly put back into our winnings for another state. In Georgia, we bought a one-dollar Mega lottery ticket, keeping the reserved six-dollar winnings to enjoy.

So, this, the Mega lottery ticket, is the one that has been sleeping in my bilfo (billfold, or as your father says, wallet) for the last eight days. Occasionally Shannan and I would casually discuss what we would do with the money if we won, i.e., she would pay off school loans and have money for graduate school, and I, on the other hand, dreamed of adding to our retirement fund the same amount of money that your father and I have paid to her university.

This morning, while your dad and I were taking our walk across the dam at the lake, I pondered why the ticket was still in my bilfo. Don't I want to know if I won? If I won, I could enjoy the benefits! If I won, then here I am continuing to live life as usual when I could be living the life of the Mega lottery winner!! Why am I waiting?

Then it came to me: as long as I do nothing, there is still a chance to win the lottery and fulfill my dreams. I will always have that chance! However, once I check the ticket, that's it. My dream of having "the winning ticket" is either fulfilled or over. So, I keep the ticket and keep the dream alive. Just think, I *have a chance to win the lottery*! And this ticket, here in my bilfo, proves it!

Then a thought comes to me—am I treating God's promises like this lottery ticket? As long as I do not cash in on his promises, I still have a chance for *big things* to happen with God. Things hoped for and all of that. But as soon as I put the faith thing on the line, there I am: either God comes through for me or he doesn't. What if he doesn't? Then I go back to my mediocre Christian life, only without the hope of greater things shall ye do[40]. Isn't that what I am afraid of? Living my life without the hope of the greater things?

Using God like a genie or a Santa Claus didn't achieve the big things in my life. That's no good. God doesn't seem to take commands from me. I wonder why he doesn't understand that I should know what's best for me and for his work; after all, it is *my* life, and I am right here and can see what is happening in *his* church! Although as I think back on it, there are some requests, both major and minor, that I am glad he didn't grant! My life could have really gotten complicated. And there have been some surprising events that have happened along the way that I very much appreciate, blessings perhaps?

What are the promises or lottery tickets that I would cash in on if I truly believed in winning God's lottery? If I believed that every ticket of faith was a winner? That to receive the blessing, all I had to do was cash it in. How would I live my life if I put faith on the line with God— meeting the criteria for the promise, and trusting him for the value and the outcome of each ticket—and just went ahead and cashed into his lottery system? Am I just unable to see beyond the material into the spiritual?

There is a popular movie that impresses on me the concept of my material earthly life versus my spiritual earthly life. In the movie, *The Matrix*, people lived what they thought were real lives while in reality they were hooked up to a material system with a simulated existence and a phony future. Of course, there were others who

---

[40] John 14:12

had been enlightened and lived separately, although at times they had to exist and interact in the simulated world.

In my current material, modern Christianity, I wonder how much I have been blinded by my worldly simulated existence. How do I get unhooked from the earthly simulated world and plugged into the real world, while staying connected? How do I become enlightened? Where is the source? How do I learn to access power? Is there a user's manual, perhaps?

Enlightenment: A couple of days ago in Florida, at Shannan's campus house, I opened my Bible at random, asking God for a scripture. I know, I know, not a good idea for disciplined study, but anyway, my eyes fell on the passage about Stephen being stoned by the angry crowd. What impressed me was that before one single rock hit him, "Stephen, full of the Holy Spirit, looked up to heaven and saw the glory of God. 'Look,' he said, 'I see heaven open and the Son of Man standing at the right hand of God'"[41].

Source: At the time of his vision, Stephen was not injured; he was not having a near-death experience or even a death experience. He was very much alive and full of Holy Spirit. *He was like me!* And so, even if I do not always see heaven open with these earthly eyes, can I see spiritually? Have I become blinded to the role of Holy Spirit? Is this person of the Trinity, this Spirit, needed for me to make a difference in the world of souls around me?

Power: Paul prayed for the Ephesians that God would give them "the spirit of wisdom and revelation in the knowledge of Him, the

---
[41] Acts 7:55 NIV

eyes of your understanding being enlightened; that you may know what is the hope of his calling, what are the riches of the glory of His inheritance in the saints, and what is the exceeding greatness of his power to usward as who believe, according to the working of his mighty power which he worked in Christ, when he raised Him from the dead, and seated Him at His own right hand in the heavenly places..."[42]. Paul goes to say that "God raised us up with Christ and seated us with him in the heavenly realms in Christ Jesus... For we are God's workmanship, created in Christ Jesus to do good works, which God prepared in advance for us to do"[43].

Manual: Isn't that what God's Word is, a manual for what to do to live an abundant life? Is this perhaps God's lottery system, a book of promises? What am I going to do? Can I trust the Creator? Can I trust the one who sent Jesus, his son, to earth to die a brutal death for me, so I could be with him for eternity? "For God so loved the world, that he gave his only begotten Son, that whosoever believeth in him should not perish, but have everlasting life"[44]. Paul says, "When you believed, you were marked in him with a seal, the promised Holy Spirit, who is a deposit, guaranteeing our inheritance..."[45].

Enlightenment, source, power, and a user's manual: Does it not then make sense for me to trust? Can I trust? Dare I trust? Dare I *not* trust? How can I apply this to my life? Paul exhorted the Ephesians in chapters 4 to 6 to live as children of light, submit to

---

[42] Ephesians 1:17–20 NKJV
[43] Ephesians 2:6–10 NIV
[44] John 3:16 KJV
[45] Ephesians 1:13–14 NIV

one another out of reverence for Christ, and "Finally, be strong in the Lord and in his mighty power. Put on the full armor of God so that you can take your stand against the devil's schemes... And pray in the Spirit on all occasions with all kinds of prayers and requests. With this in mind, be alert and always keep on praying for all the Lord's people"[46].

I feel compelled to no longer throw away or ignore the Godly lottery tickets but to put on the full armor of God, and as a workmanship of God, I am not at the mercy of an earthy lottery system. I am depending on the faithfulness of the treasury system of the Promise Bank of Heaven, "the riches of his glorious inheritance" [47]. I am challenged to live my life by putting *all* of my faith on the line with God. I want to trust him for the value and the outcome of my faith, not just in this simulated earthly existence but in the spiritual, which is real life – immortality.

As I sit here, I am reminded of when you passed on, and I was told that if only I had had more faith, you would not have died. As I stood then and said, I will stand now and say, "I must have faith in my God, not faith in my faith." I am called into his glorious inheritance! I get to share in *Christ's inheritance*! Because I depend on his faith, it is not from me, it is the gift of God![48] I set out again today to continue to stand and have faith in my God. Not just with some of my Godly lottery tickets, or promises, but with as many promises as he gives me the grace in which to grow.

---

46 Ephesians 6:10, 18 NIV
47 Ephesians 1:18b NIV
48 Ephesians 2:8 NIV

The Book of Numbers in the Bible states that "God is not human that he should lie, not a human being, that he should change his mind. Does he speak and then not act? Does he promise and not fulfill? I have received a command to bless; he has blessed, and I cannot change it"[49]. Therefore, I must not throw away my confidence, for it will be richly rewarded. I must persevere so that when I have done the will of God, I will receive what He has promised[50]. I pray that the Lord God helps me to see things as he would have me see them and to do his will in the life that he has given me.

Love, Mom

---

49 Numbers 23:19–20 NIV
50 Hebrews 10:35-36 NIV

They May Be Buzzards, But They Can Fly

September 5, 2008
Cincinnati

Dear Nathan,

Early September, and I'm enjoying the morning at the lake after completing my walk. I'm sitting in the truck waiting for your father to finish his jog. With my arms propped up on the open window, I lean out and look up. Catching the updraft over the top of the dam are twelve to fifteen buzzards with their wings spread wide, facing into the wind. It's one of those mornings that welcome a perfect, balmy, seventy-degree breeze after a humid summer of nineties-plus. Although flying, the buzzards appear stationary in the opposing wind. Slowly, one by one, the buzzards, being swept back, exert just the barest effort to again line up with the rest. About ten feet above the surface of the dam, looking lakeside and off across the glittering morning light on the water and into the woods beyond, there they are, just drifting. "They are buzzards! But they can fly! They are just having fun and enjoying the morning."

Imagine that! God gave even buzzards something peaceful and relaxing to do on a random Friday morning. Why did he do that?

To give them some joy in their otherwise very messy lives? If God cares this much for his scavengers, why do I allow myself to stress out? Why do I not totally relax as they seem to be doing in this God-given moment? Well, Nathan, maybe I'm like your father, who is becoming a little bit irritated with these same buzzards as he comes jogging by. He doesn't seem to appreciate the commentary they are evidently making on his jogging!

Rick has at least weekly, for the past fifteen years, jogged across both dams on this road at the lake. Any time he sees a vulture flying way up above, he will yell out to them in a screechy call between singing verses of his favorite song for this setting. "Big birds flyin' across the sky, throwin' shadows on our eyes", *Helpless* by Neil Young [51]. Usually, he runs casually and carefree with arms spread wide as the big bird will circle lower and lower, but not too close, wide circles at a pleasant distance just close enough to enjoy the musical entertainment.

But this time something is different about your father's singing. He is beginning to wave his arms and mutter. Now he is yelling at the buzzards above him! The buzzards, however, are undaunted as more and more of them abandon their lazy drifting, yelling at their buddies. "There he goes, Zeke!" "Hey, Buzz, look!" "Yard, here's our troubadour!" "Come on, guys, maybe he'll recognize us!" They begin to follow your father along the road at the top of the dam. I kid you not! They really are. And he really is yelling and waving his arms! Buzzards are hovering now, not more than four to six feet above his head. They're still catching the updraft of the wind

---

[51] "Helpless," by Neil Young 1970

current over the top of the dam, but now they are flying along with your father, just the windward tips of their wings fluttering. They are graceful; you can say that about them—the buzzards, that is, not your father, who is getting more and more desperate. He must be thinking of the next lines of the song as he beats the rhythm onto the guardrail with one hand and waves his fist at the buzzards with the other. I bet this has indeed left him feeling helpless, like the songwriter, because he is now waving at me to pick him up in the truck. Guess I better go get him.

Wanting to leave a situation, as your dad was, reminds me of Apostle Paul expressing the same attitude, not out of fear but maybe because of some frustration yet also anticipation of heaven. He said, "I desire to depart and be with Christ, which is better by far; but it is more necessary for you that I remain in the body"[52]. But, for me, is it frustration and stress that I am expressing when I moan and complain to God? Sometimes when I'm tired of running and the buzzards are arriving one by one. And I'm not talking about Rick's groupie buzzards like Zeke, Buzz, Yard and the rest.

Circling buzzards wouldn't be so bad, at least they would be way off and waiting, but when they seem so close and ready to do something... What do I think the buzzards of this life are really going to do? Do I really think that I am easy pickings for the enemy? Did God give them the nature (i.e., power) to harm me as long as I continue to run? Sure, it's irritating as it was to your father, but is it really risky as long as I continue to run the race or walk the walk of faith? After which there will be in store for me a

---

[52] Philippians 1:23b-24 NIV

crown of righteousness[53]. Don't I have to lie down and give up to be buzzard bait?

What's my assurance of safety in this faith walk? Will God protect me from the buzzards in my life? Jesus gave us this assurance when he prayed for protection for his disciples. He asked the Father to include those who *will* believe in him in the future[54]. God's protection also extends into eternity. Scripture in Hebrews says that "God is not unjust; he will not forget your work and the love you have shown him as you have helped his people and continue to help them. We want each of you to show this same diligence to the very end, so that what you hope for may be fully realized"[55].

In regard to the certainty of God's promise, Hebrews also says, "We have this hope as an anchor for the soul, firm and secure"[56]. I like the sound of that; it's poetry to my heart: "an anchor for the soul, firm and secure." If I knew nothing else, this alone would certainly keep me from giving up, lying down and becoming buzzard bait! Wait a minute—which way am I going here as I write? Peace and Restoration or How Not to Become Buzzard Bait? It's tempting to go off in both directions, but my purpose here is to focus on God in his mercy, creating things to enjoy and giving us the ability to enjoy them, to be restored and not stressed. I do admit that not seeing oneself as buzzard bait is a sight more peaceful; however, tune in at a later date for my thoughts on buzzard bait.

---

53 2 Timothy 4:7–8
54 John 17:6–20
55 Hebrews 6:10–11 NIV
56 Hebrews 6:19 NIV

Back to stress-free living... If I just spend my time and energy collecting material possessions, it increases the stress in my life. God commands me not to put my hope in wealth "but to put their hope in God who richly provides us with everything for our enjoyment"[57]. God made everything to enjoy: the earth, the stars, and the planets, and yes, this also includes the wind patterns as well. How loving. "As you do not know the path of the wind, or how the body is formed in a mother's womb, so you cannot understand the work of God, the Maker of all things"[58].

While watching the buzzards enjoy the beautiful balmy breeze—that is, the path of the wind over the top of the dam at the lake—I recall Jesus's comment regarding sparrows. Even though they aren't worth much, "not one of them is forgotten by God... Don't be afraid; you are worth more than many sparrows"[59]. In the Old Testament, God had expressed to Jonah a concern for the many animals as well as the people of Nineveh[60]. Although we are worth much more to him, God still cares for his birds, and yes, even his buzzards.

When I'm looking up on an autumn morning, watching the drifting birds overhead, I think, "They're just buzzards!" But God, the Creator, sees some of his creation and cares enough to give the scavengers rest and relaxation on a September morning. Perhaps God in his mercy gives buzzards the panoramic view for a bit of

---

57 1 Timothy 6:17b NIV
58 Ecclesiastes 11:5 NIV
59 Luke 12:6–7 NIV
60 Jonah 4:11

enjoyment. I suppose I would need a different perspective at times if it were my job to stick my head into carcasses. Can you imagine?

Huh? What's that? As a Christ follower, is that what God called me to do? Get up close and personal with those who are distressed and dying in spiritual darkness, needing life-giving light or those trapped in the troubles of the world? Are you sure? Carcass can be defined as "remains from which the substance or character is gone"[61]. Sounds like all of humanity prior to God's light! But then God gives us his light. Matthew records Jesus telling them and now us, "Ye are the light of the world… Let your light so shine before men, that they may see your good works, and glorify your Father which is in heaven[62]. Is this what Jesus did when he came from Perfection to live among us in human flesh? Am I supposed to get involved in the decaying lives of those around me? Jesus taught the disciples that a faithful and wise servant will be doing what he has been put in charge to do[63].

Do? Do what? This is what I ask Jesus as did the disciples when rebuked for seeking after him to satisfy only their earthly needs instead of the eternal. "What must we do to do the works God requires?" Jesus answered, "The work of God is this: to believe in the one he has sent"[64]. Apostle Paul wrote in Ephesians "For you were once darkness, but now you are light in the Lord. Live as children of light (for the fruit of the light consists in all goodness, righteousness and truth,) and find out what pleases the Lord"[65].

---

[61] American Heritage Dictionary 5th Edition
[62] Mathew 5:14, 16
[63] Matthew 24:45–46
[64] John 6:28–29 NIV
[65] Ephesians 5:8–10 NIV

Then a few verses later he wrote "Do not be foolish but understand what the Lord's will is. Do not get drunk on wine, which leads to debauchery. Instead, be filled with the Spirit, speaking to one another with psalms, hymns, and songs from the Spirit. Sing and make music in your heart to the Lord, always giving thanks to God the Father for everything, in the name of our Lord Jesus Christ"[66]. Am I a light in the darkness of this world? How do I choose what to get involved in with so much going on around me?

When choosing what we are to do for God, Paul gives us some very good advice: "Be very careful, then, how you live, not as unwise but as wise, making the most of every opportunity, because the days are evil[67]. Is this perhaps also a secret to soaring stress free like the buzzards above the dam on a balmy September morning? Am I to do those good works that God wants me to do instead of just the ones I'm *willing* to do? Am I not only to commune with him, feed on the manna of His Word, and fellowship with other believers, but also do good works that he has prepared for me?

Then, when the winds of life blow a little extra hard on me, I need only to exert the barest effort to again line up with my family in Christ. I have sought to do this with all the losses I've sustained, and I pray that, with God's grace, I have succeeded. If nothing else, I've gained wisdom, hard won through experience, having learned that facing pain and overcoming hardship grants us a keener perspective on what does and does not matter in life. This is part of having

---

[66] Ephesians 5:17–20 NIV
[67] Ephesians 5:15–16 NIV

unconditional faith, which only comes through true acceptance and true surrender.

The loss of you in our lives, Nathan, was more like a hurricane force threatening to blow us off our spiritual course. However, with the peace of God in my heart and faith in his faithfulness, I know there are still good works for me to do here on earth. This allows me the opportunity, like the buzzards this balmy September morning, to also be able to enjoy God's creation as I relax, stress free, at the top of the dam, looking lakeside and off across the glittering morning light on the water and into the woods beyond. I can drift in my thoughts for a moment and think, "They are buzzards! But they can fly! We are *all* just having fun and enjoying the morning, no matter what our assignment in life!"

So glad you enjoyed the morning with me, Nathan! And although I appreciate the capacity of buzzards *to rise above it all and fly* "... those who hope in the LORD will renew their strength. They will soar on wings like eagles; they will run and not grow weary, they will walk and not be faint"[68].

Yes, I hear a higher, stronger call to continually endeavor, no matter what comes, not to be limited to the strength of buzzards but *rise up and fly as with wings of eagles!*

Love, Mom

---

[68] Isaiah 40:31 NIV

Hay Canyon

August 4, 2010
Sacramento, NM

Dear Nathan,

This past February, a snowstorm, a narrow country road, and an oncoming vehicle combined to send your father on his way to join you. As rescuers surrounded me alongside that snowy roadside, the new world that I had come to know since you left us, lay in ruins. I was forced once again onto an unknown path. This new journey began with eight months of much pain, hospitals, and physical rehabilitation for me. I not only had to learn to walk again physically, but also to walk again emotionally and spiritually. As you would have expected, knowing your little sister as you do, Shannan provided not only the necessary care, but also loving support and encouragement as we both journeyed along our individual paths to emotional recovery and, for me, physical recovery as well.

I have progressed from stretcher to wheelchair to walker and now to a cane! With me still unable to work, Shannan and I decided to spend the summer in the mountains of New Mexico. Since I had grown up in New Mexico, your dad and I had planned to relocate this summer to my home state's open spaces and wide blue skies. So it was only natural for Shannan and me, during our first summer without your dad, to get away to the New Mexico mountains to continue to recuperate. I am walking daily up the mountain road. And at an elevation of 7,500 feet, that is a workout, even for the short distance I walk.

We have rented a cabin in Hay Canyon next door to a couple who were two of our youth leaders in Carlsbad when I was a teenager. They have been such a blessing to us this summer. Guests have been frequent here at our cabin in the mountains. They come from as close as Carlsbad, New Mexico, two hours away every weekend, to as far away as Florida for our big event when the Orlando group all came up. We had such a great time with a memorable road trip to the City of Rocks in Western New Mexico; on to Arizona to visit Tombstone, the Grand Canyon, and Antelope Canyon; and then to Utah's Monument Valley. Just before getting back to Hay Canyon in the Sacramento Mountains, we crossed the Valley of Fire lava flow in the Tularosa Basin. I had so much fun!

We all had a blast and took a great many pictures of Hournbuckles taking pictures of Hournbuckles taking pictures. Ha-ha. You would have loved the whole adventure, although I am sure it doesn't compare to what you have been experiencing in heaven! And thinking yourself to the many galaxies as well!

Love, Mom

Eighteen Years in Eternity Plus One

February 9, 2011
Cincinnati

Dear Nathan,

I can hardly believe that you have now been living in the forever hereafter for almost nineteen years. Here it seems like only yesterday that you left. Although I know you are no longer bound by time, I wonder if you were surprised last year when your father joined you there. I also wonder if your dad talked with you regarding the circumstances of that journey. I can only relate to you the details from my own earthly perspective as I described in my last letter about Hay Canyon.

As with many new journeys around the holidays, the path of grief is often heavy with old memories, days now lost, and yet these memories are accompanied by fresh new pain. So this past Christmas, Shannan and I decided not to face the holiday in familiar surroundings without the familiarity of your father's presence.

The previous year, one of my brothers and his family spent Christmas with us here in Cincinnati. Since his wife was facing the same situation after my brother Paul's journey to heaven, a short three months after your dad's, we girls decided to go together on a European holiday. So off we went, the four of us, Shannan and I, along with your aunt and her daughter. We went to London for Christmas and to Paris for New Year's! We still missed all of you, but we had an amazing time building new holiday memories to bridge the gap of our greatest losses and to travel into our personal tomorrows here below.

Miss you still,
Love, Mom

Moving Right Along

August 24, 2012
Carlsbad, New Mexico

Dear Nathan,

I decided to retire from practice as a nurse practitioner, although I will be online faculty for the University of Cincinnati. I moved to my hometown in New Mexico this summer and live next door to the house I grew up in where one of my brothers and his wife now live. They had moved into the family home to care for your Grandpa five years ago, and last year we had to move Grandpa into a nursing home. Were you surprised when he recently joined you in heaven? I was glad to be close by his last summer here. Another brother of mine is here and will soon be moving his family back to New Mexico around Thanksgiving. He is looking for a place in New Mexico's Sacramento Mountains.

We are all keeping very busy renovating properties we own. Whew, that's hard work; be glad you got a mansion prepared for you by Jesus![69] I remember how you and Shannan used to tease me that

---

[69] John 14:2-3 some versions say, "many rooms in my Father's house". I'm using KJV and NKJV here for the purpose of this discussion.

if you get to heaven first, you will help Jesus build my mansion and will put ceramic geese in clothes on the porch so I will know which mansion is mine. I would reply in disgust, "Oh, no you won't!" Knowing how I hated seeing dressed-up geese lounging on porches, you would reply with a laugh, "Oh yes! I will!" Living in the country, this was a running joke on me since we passed many such geese every Sunday on the way to church a couple of villages away. I am certainly not holding you to *that* promise.

Love, Mom

What Did You Go Out to the Desert to See?

September 28, 2012
Carlsbad, New Mexico

Dear Nathan,

Wide awake at 4:00 a.m., I decide to begin my day and work on some projects on my computer. After an initially slow connection, I am unable to open the required sites and try using my smartphone. Well, this isn't working since my smartphone knows it's too early for anything other than sleeping. My tablet must think the same, wanting to be charged prior to starting the day. I agree that is important, and being on my third cup of coffee, I again attempt to connect with the wild blue yonder with the aid of Internet connections on my laptop. Now I am getting frustrated, and the day isn't even getting light yet. It's time for another conversation with my Internet carrier.

I had specifically purchased my wireless Internet devise in Cincinnati for travel purposes in the Southwest. Irritated by a couple of weeks of slow Internet and multiple lengthy phone conversations, I now enjoy an additional ninety-minute conversation with several corporate people. Finally, today, after multiple failed attempts online at activating my new SIM card, which had been sent special delivery, I am informed that I will have to connect directly with the nearest company tower.

Being conscientious about combining trips, and it now being after eight o'clock, I decide to stop by the bank to take care of some business. Sitting in the bank parking lot, I realize that I did not bring the correct checkbook, checking card, or other information that will be required. So, another idea for a productive morning bites the dust, and the wind isn't even blowing! Anyway, *onward*! I venture forth to do my part in saving the world—sorry, I'm getting carried away—I mean, I will do my part in saving my day and follow my Internet carrier's instructions to drive across the state line into Texas on Highway 62 in order to connect with the company's very own tower.

An hour later, I'm gazing off into the near distance (Is that possible? Wouldn't that just be nearby?), admiring the beautiful view of El Capitan (Signal Peak as we called it years ago). As it nears noon, the day is heating up. I sit in my truck on a deserted desert road in Texas, wishing I had some dessert and certain that I will be successful in rebooting my desirable Internet devise if I follow the instructions I received early this morning, which did not include any advice on writing an appropriate paragraph without run-on sentences! Anyway, I try to reboot and complete the activation of my new SIM card.

Not being successful after multiple heartfelt attempts at reconnecting to the Internet via my mobile devise, I have a brilliant thought: why would a company put a cell phone tower way out here when the nearest town is El Paso, a mere 125 miles further into Texas? Oops, after careful review of my road atlas, I realize that I could have driven east into Texas farm country (think multiple farmers with cell phones at hand) instead of south into the wide Texas ranges of scarcely populated ranches. Because Highway 62 goes both east and south from Carlsbad into Texas. Maybe, just maybe, since I was not wearing my hearing aids during that early morning conversation, I just might have misheard the instructions. Food would have been a good idea for brainpower too!

Heading back to Carlsbad to take Highway 62 east instead of south and enjoying the awesome view and wondering about the purpose of my life as it relates to this particular morning, I hear an unwelcome sound. You know that "ping" accompanied by an extra light flashing on the dash in a bright color announcing that, incredibly, my morning has just gotten worse. Yep! There is nothing to improve the day like your truck overheating on a desert road at noon. At least it is a late September, 90-degree day. It could have been a hot, midsummer 114-degree day or a freak snowstorm with 70-mph wind! Well, maybe not the snowstorm.

Wishing I could have made it to at least the one and only gas station around, I coast to the side of the road, steam emanating from my hood *and* my truck's hood as well! Here I sit, looking at what is now too far of a distance in the desert to reach: Whites City. Talk about faith. One can tell by the name of that very small but quaint tourist place (2010 population of seven) that someone had great expectations when he included *City* in its name. Looks like forty-eight people from the previous census moved to the burbs. But there is still hope! Speaking of which, Hope, New Mexico (population

105), is at least on the way to the mountains instead of the cell-phone-towerless Texas desert. But back to what is going on today in the life of the unfamous Grace.

Actually, I think I am rather enjoying my time here by the side of the road, all alone but not lonesome. First, I congratulate myself because I have followed the survival skills training my mother taught me for the Southwest and currently have with me the following items: a case of water, emergency food consisting of tuna salad packs and peanut butter crackers, a first aid kit (which I now remember leaving at the house we are renovating. But my first thought was that I had it, so it counts), a bed roll, extra blankets, matches and a computer with (out) Internet service, and (I forgot to mention earlier) a cell phone that started updating itself at the Texas state line, resulting in being currently unavailable for *any* calls). Oh, and a hat and sunglasses!

In spite of everything, I'm not alone anymore because a dragonfly is now sitting on the antenna with me. Well, he is on the antenna; I am just standing here taking pictures of him from two feet away. Getting tired of the limelight, he takes flight to parts unknown. Turning my attention elsewhere, I take ground-level pictures of the grasses and flowers at the edge of the road. I do, however, stand up with the camera visible each time a car approaches on the road. I don't want anyone thinking that I am squatting down in the grass and bushes for other reasons—you know, like picking wildflowers!

I do notice something though: the further I get from my truck with its raised hood, and the more down to earth I get, the more the beauty of the wildflowers and grasses are visible and the less prominent my stalled truck. Hmm, wonder if there is a life lesson here somewhere? I will have to ponder that question on another early morning or during downtime. Oh, good, here comes my brother with lunch and additional water for my radiator (cell phone was back online earlier). After unsuccessful efforts to deal with the overheated engine but good conversation in my brother's truck for forty-five minutes, we wait for the tow truck to arrive. Now, grateful to be getting back to Carlsbad, I find out from the garage personnel that they won't be able to even look at my truck for another week! But, hey, at least they are letting me park on their lot!

As I ponder the possible life lessons from today's little jaunt into the desert, I see several productive directions. I could discuss being equipped for spiritual survival— forgiveness of all wrongdoing, bread of life, sword of the Spirit, and emergency plan for my forever-after. Or I could even discuss how giving myself permission to see beauty, although not removing the trial, allows me to survive without despair. But the phrase that keeps going through my mind is a question Jesus had asked the crowds concerning John the Baptist. He was clarifying the differences between the expectations of the crowd versus the reality of the prophet and his message.

"What did you go out to the desert to see?"[70] Because I had misunderstood the message from my Internet carrier, the results of my drive into the desert today were vastly different from my expectations. How do my expectations impact how I live my reality? As a Christ follower, is it reasonable to expect an overcoming life to be one without sorrow and loss? When Jesus prayed for his

---

70 Matthew 11:7 NIV

followers, he did not ask the Father to keep them from evil or disaster but from the Evil one. "I am not asking you to take them out of the world but to keep them safe from the evil one. They don't belong to the world, just as I don't belong to the world. Make them ready for your service through your truth; your teaching is truth. I have sent them into the world, just as you sent me into the world. For their sake I am making myself ready, to serve so they can be ready for their service of truth"[71].

What did I go out to the desert of life to see? I never expected to live without trouble, but I also never expected to see the loss of a child, maybe eventually my husband but certainly not one of my children. The reality is that through these journeys I have indeed needed the spiritual survival skills my mother taught me, and I have also had to focus on the beauty of my life here without the two of you. However, the less I focus on the moments of your deaths, the more visible is the beauty of your new lives in your ever-after. And of necessity I have had to also acknowledge the man and his message—both of John the Baptist, "Repent for the kingdom of God is at hand,"[72] and of Jesus the Christ, "Make them ready for your service through your truth; your teaching is truth"[73].

Love, Mom

---

[71] John 17:15–19 NCV
[72] Matthew 3:1-2 NKJV
[73] John 17:17 NCV

Imperfection

October 13, 2013
Cincinnati

Dear Nathan,

It's too cool to enjoy the early morning outside. No sitting on the deck under an umbrella in the rain at Shannan's house in Cincinnati…waiting for first light. So, moving into the sunroom, I settle into the grandma chair with Puma, Shannan's dog. Due to her coloring (the dog's, not Shannan's), she was so named after we spent the summer of 2010 in the Sacramento Mountains of southern New Mexico—nights of hearing the screaming of elusive pumas.

Anyway, back to this morning. Sitting here in the sunroom having morning devotions, I'm reading examples in the Bible of people who, although imperfect, were used by God to accomplish wonderful, marvelous works. Having just yesterday concluded that I had to do something about my overwhelming tendency to avoid dealing with my finances, I was feeling very inadequate. However, today, considering these people and the fact that they still were used to accomplish great things, I rest easier knowing that I am not totally off God's usefulness list, especially since accomplishments depend on God's creativity instead of any possible perfection in me.

I used to be able to juggle the numbers and thrived on financial info. I enjoyed making charts of everything coming in and going out. I could spend many happy hours charting the course of family finances, and I loved numbers. I blossomed whenever a number or account problem surfaced, but not now. I'm sort of like the plant that is watching me type. It was in full bloom on my last visit. Now it is smaller and less attractive yet sitting there on the side table as if it is something special. Elevated to a better place than the outside deck, in spite of its stem being all dried up, this plant still has the strength to unfold fresh new leaves.

Like the plant, can I really begin new growth in a different direction right now? Hey, I can't even seem to muster enough self-discipline to care about managing my finances. I would rather be pulling weeds, tiling floors, digging fencepost holes by chipping through New Mexico rock, or just knocking down some walls in 'rehab joy'. I'd do anything but focus on obscene mail. You know, the envelopes with see-through panels. The ones that I tend to avoid because it would require me to sit down and attend to financial business.

Will Creator God really be willing to move me to a new place when I am not fully involved in my now stuff, and with my very evident inadequacies in discipline? I spoke to Chester, one of my younger brothers, who has observed my struggle over the last year and just yesterday strongly suggested that I ask for assistance from Lewis, my numbers-gifted accountant older brother. Outsourcing what is mundane for me to someone gifted and who can appreciate and enjoy numbers: an accountant, *yes*! Younger suggested that I focus on *my* gifts, not past interests or strengths. Oh, but it's hard to admit that I don't need to do it all, that another direction might be in order, that I don't need to bog myself down with what is no longer compelling to me.

Instead, I should lend myself to other things, other ways to creatively express myself, as in attending to my use of run-on sentences.

Recently, as an aspiring author, I was advised to blog. Can I really begin as suggested and open a blog? Can I understand the mystery of the blog? I had never until yesterday even known the definition of blog, much less read a blog! Hey, I find myself needing to discipline myself in self-discipline in order to be disciplined. How can I slog through this seeming "mind field"? Blogging mind field? Mind blogging?

Here I sit in the sunroom this autumn morning, thinking about blogs while looking at the dried-up plant elevated to a better position and bravely putting on new growth. Time ticks on as I ponder examples of old-time heroes, heroes who are inadequate and flawed like the plant but still willing to let the hand of Creator God chart a new course. So as instructed, I'm composing my very first blog entry: Imperfection. Although inadequate in my humanness, I trust that my own imperfect journey inspires those who read your conversational poem and my Dear Nathan letters to walk their own path with faith in God our Father and with the peace of our Lord Jesus Christ.

Love, Mom

Avoidance

October 28, 2013
Cincinnati

Dear Nathan,

I mentioned my attachment to avoidance in my last letter, entitled "Imperfection". Initially I thought that outsourcing would be the best way to deal with avoidance of my finances. It sounds really good, outsourcing sounds productive. You know, give the stack of stuff to someone more knowledgeable and qualified and forge on to fun, exciting pursuits. Reminds me of a *Seinfeld* TV episode I once saw. The character's financial filing system was a big manila envelope overstuffed with pieces of paper, bills, and statements jumbled together as if just gathered up from the floor where it had been previously spilled. He couldn't understand his accountant's dismay and reluctance.

When I consider consulting Creator God about my stuff, it's interesting that I seem to have the opposite reaction from the sitcom character consulting his accountant. I think that I have to gather all the scattered pieces of my life, organize them in a filing system that makes sense to me, and with a game plan in place, *then* ask

Father God to step in and help me achieve the success I envision. After all, who knows more about me and my life than I? It's okay to ask him for help, but I want to keep my rights to it all, you know… my creative rights…just to make sure that my life goes according to plan.

Hmm, my plan, my creative rights… Creator God! I honestly did not see that coming. Am I looking at everything backward? Is it really Creator God…creative rights…his plan?

Do I really think that I have creative rights to my life? Am I the pot looking at the potter[74] and saying, "Why did you make me this way? I wanted to be and do something else or sit on a different shelf in a different place!" "I want" is all about what I am thinking and feeling at the moment—sounds a little two-year-oldish, doesn't it? I demand that motorcycle *now* to ride over a cliff just like on that TV show! But all I hear is "No". Then, sounding a little more grown up—say maybe six, sixteen, or for some of us, sixty years old—I spout, "I hate you," a phrase every parent, including Father God, has heard at least once.

Maybe the sitcom character had it right to begin with. Hand over the mess to someone who knows what to do with it. Who better to outsource to than an expert, someone who can look at all of those little bits and pieces of my life that I have tried unsuccessfully to stuff in my manila envelope? Hand it over to someone who knows what to discard, what to file till later, and what to deal with now—someone who knows the blueprint for my life. The Psalmist wrote,

---

74 Romans 9:20-22

"Many, Lord my God, are the wonders you have done, the things you planned for us. None can compare with you; were I to speak and to tell of your deeds, they would be too many to declare" [75]. Outsource to an expert to advise me in my day-to-day existence. Someone who knows which step I should take in this life of endless and incredible possibilities. Another Psalm says, "Your word is a lamp for my feet, a light on my path" [76].

A pastor of ours, Rev. Dr. R. Edgar Bonniwell, once said, "The Christian life is the most exciting life of all because you never know when God is going to abrogate your plans and take you off on an exciting adventure."

My life experiences have certainly proven that to be the case. Through every adventure—a word I'm using collectively to describe pain and joy, heartache and wonder, loss and renewal—I came to discover that faith alone sustains. If I had succumbed to avoidance after losing you, Nathan, I would have lost my way and not been able to survive the loss of you. Acceptance is the opposite of avoidance, and through true acceptance and the surrender to God it demands, we cultivate enduring faith.

Love, Mom

---

[75] Psalm 40:5 NIV
[76] Psalm 119:105 NIV

Beautiful on the Mountains Are Feet

November 22, 2013
Cincinnati

Dear Nathan,

What is it about feet? Unless they are booted, dressed up with stylish shoes or adorned with nail polish and jewels, we tend to ignore them. Some of us blatantly display them as if they are really something or because they are nothing. Maybe we keep them covered in modesty or because we feel vulnerable or think that our feet are ugly and that we should hide them. Or perhaps we never consider them at all, other than as something on which to strap the latest footgear. Do we take them for granted as they keep plodding along taking us in the direction we are headed? And is there really a purpose to the direction other than just meeting each day as it comes, one step at a time?

Sometimes, I live my life as if I am still stuck in the crowd at Buckingham Palace waiting for the changing of the guard as I was in December 2010. Maybe I stay where I am in life, because like then, I'm just stuck in the crowd unable to visualize where to go or how to progress toward my future. I can't fathom what everyone else in anticipation observes beyond the obstacles. Is there something purposeful beyond this crowd?

What do they view from where they are near the gate? Or does it really matter that my feet are just standing behind them, trying to grasp what everyone else is doing? Just feet really, nothing special, walking or standing, what does it matter? Then focusing on the only thing I can see and looking up to other people, just like taking a picture, I try to adjust my exposure, change the contrast… anything! But it seems just like that day in London. The crowd wait in expectation while all that is apparent to me are snippets of their lives. All I can see are essentially like the elbows, a purse, and someone's face looking forward that I viewed back then. But what are they looking forward too? I try adjusting the color of this photograph in life and look at everything differently hoping it helps—but it doesn't. I still can't envision possibilities for my own life.

I know I am here for a purpose, but the end sight escapes me. Oh well, there's nothing to do but focus on me and look down at my purple-booted feet as I did back then, when they were taking me nowhere. And like then, I am stuck right here in the same old place, with nowhere to go. Well, I might as well make a good impression while I'm here, in case anyone is looking. So, as I did at the Palace, I adjust my pose and socialize a bit. Or maybe a new look and crowd is just what I need and forget about direction and purpose. Wish it were possible to propel myself through this mass of humanity to somewhere else away from the gates holding us back!

Or is there a higher calling to where my feet should be taking me? Feet booted up or painted and bejeweled for the public, do they all need embellishment to be beautiful? Should I hide or display my feet? Are they ugly or a canvas for rugged or decorative sandals and toe rings? Or maybe I should be private and modest when it comes to my feet. Is their only purpose to take me along whatever path I happen to find myself on? I wonder what Creator God would say. Would he present a technical creator viewpoint, discussing phalanges and ligaments? Or does he perhaps view the beauty of our feet based on where they take us and what we do with our opportunities? In scripture, the Prophet Isaiah said "How beautiful on the mountains are the feet of those who bring good news, who proclaim peace, who bring good tidings, who proclaim salvation, who say to Zion, 'Your God reigns'"[77].

Nathan, over the years since you have departed this earth, my feet have walked the path of my journey of faith, as I've described in my letters to you. Feet obviously play a significant role in walking, but in a walk of faith, the path is very important. Although your path to heaven preceded mine, Jesus has been ever beside me as I journey here below and strive to bring the good news of how anyone can meet you over there.

Love, Mom

---

[77] Isaiah 52:7 NIV

Assumptions

December 2, 2013
Cincinnati

Dear Nathan,

I'm sitting here in the sunroom experiencing the warmth and beauty of my new space heater, which is allowing me to comfortably enjoy this winter morning. I found a really cute but functional heater that is just the thing. It has the look of a cast-iron stove with hot coals and flickering flames. I know, I know, isn't it funny what one will do for a little bit of the real thing? It's not really a fire in my little heater, but I do have warmth, and it fits conveniently into the available space. Hmm, perhaps that's why it's called a "space heater"? It's cute and functional but does have what I consider a rather bothersome and somewhat unattractive feature: a large white label attached to the cord near the plug. Really, it doesn't even blend into the decor! Not that it matters. After all, the label *is* located near the end of the cord, so it's partially hidden behind the end table, but it's annoying and ugly just the same! I am a visual person; I like to tweak and tweak, constantly adjusting this and that to achieve the most perfect look. I don't admit even to myself that since I use imperfect objects in imperfect situations, all I really achieve for my efforts is imperfection. I also totally ignore the fact that I am imperfect and therefore have imperfect ideas and ideals. However, leaving the subject of imperfection behind for another day, I am driven to tweak my surroundings this winter morning.

I reach for the offending tag behind the end table and am confronted with shouts in large bold letters: *Avertissement pour reduire leisqué d'incendie: ne pas retirer cette etiquette!* What? I turn the tag over and again it shouts, *"Warning to reduce the risk of fire: do not remove this tag!"* Responding automatically, I scoff, "Yeah, right, as if leaving this tag on is going to reduce the risk of fire! Someone would have to read and follow the fine print on the tag to reduce the risk of fire, not just leave the tag in place!" I stalk off to get a snack to enjoy while sitting in the now warm sunroom.

Sulking, I think, "Another example of a dumb tag, just like the one on the space heater I bought last winter." That tag supposedly gave guidance for choosing the right heater for the space. No dimensions were given, just pictures of different size squares that were labeled large, medium, and small, so I could choose a large, medium, or small heater to fit a large, medium, or small room. Sitting back down with a snack all arranged, I decide that it would probably be a good idea to read the entire warning label. This is when I realize that I had assumed that what I thought I read was what the tag actually said. Maybe I need to do a little tweaking to my thinking as well.

Taking time to read the fine print, I realize now that I had totally ignored the colon in the tag's phrase. Such a little thing really, but how it changes the meaning of what I had thought it said. Webster defines colon as a punctuation mark used chiefly to direct attention to matter (as a list, explanation, quotation, or amplification) that follows. The colon directed attention to a list of instructions on how to reduce the risk of fire. The final statement, "Leave tag in place," was an admonition to leave the warning tag in place for all who would make use of the space heater in the future. It was not only for the initial installer of the space heater but also for all of those to follow. I should not assume I know what was meant without reading the details of the instructions. Instead of assumptions, when I take the time to read further and gain more understanding, I am indeed doing as Proverbs advises, "The wise store up knowledge"[78].

The truly wise increase their knowledge of spiritual matters. Nathan, your wisdom at age eight has illuminated my path throughout all the years that have followed since your passing. It is said that the wisdom of children humbles and inspires all of us; that has certainly been the case for me where you're concerned!

Love, Mom

---

78 Proverbs 10:14a NIV

2013-2015
Concluding the Matter

Concluding the Matter are my further musings on moving forward and my reassessment of previous conclusions I had made after Nathan passed away. It also reflects my thoughts at the time of publishing the first edition of this book and additional thoughts on the subject of death since then.

Vapors – An Incentive to Move Forward

Nov 5, 2023

Note to Reader,

While preparing the second edition of this *Mars* book My computer assistant informs me that the first word in the original title for this letter might offend some readers and suggests I choose a different word. My title for this chapter in the first edition was "Fart, then Move On". Butt... oh sorry.... *But* I liked that title. It was both more descriptive and clearly informative for an appropriate reaction. I think it is helpful when experiencing an unexpected event, to then be able to immediately identify a solution. Now searching online for a synonym my computer assistant will approve, the most interesting word replacement for "fart" I find is "vapors". So there you have it, my alternative title. (I had to laugh out loud!)

December 30, 2013
Cincinnati

Dear Nathan,

I realize as I lie here awake who should have filled the empty chair to my right at last Friday night's dinner party. Seven ladies had had dinner at a friend's newly renovated home. Now, tonight, I'm thinking that the woman at Shannan's dinner party last evening should have filled the chair left vacant at the Friday-night dinner. I do not know what exactly the correct term for this woman and my new relatedness is; however, Shannan now calls her mother-in-law. I do know, however, that she and I share more than our children. After all, just three days ago she brought me home at five thirty in the morning. Shannan, still jetlagged, had come home earlier with my car.

This newly related woman and I entered the house through the garage on the lower level. She had steadied me as I walked shakily into the laundry room and promptly threw up for the third time that night. Being as quiet as we could so as not to wake our grown kids, she had, before leaving, insisted on making sure that I was settled comfortably in bed in my own private area of the house on the garage level. Still nauseated and woozy, I wondered why anyone would spend any time in such a state, even for the sake of a night out on the town. I, however, owed my situation to a late night of hospital induced nausea and vomiting from the potions and motions of technological advancements and diagnostics. The current situation was not necessarily an improvement to the severe abdominal pain that had sent me to the emergency room in the first place at nine o'clock on Christmas night.

This same pain has been my constant companion for the past twelve days. And alas, even after an Urgent Care visit earlier last week and the emergency room visit on Christmas night, this is why I am up shortly after midnight typing my thoughts and trying not to focus on my abdomen. Three days ago, shortly after midnight on Christmas, I sent first Shannan from my hospital bedside and later my new son-in-law home to catch up on much needed sleep. They had just returned from Europe on Christmas Eve. The jet-lagged couple had honeymooned in Prague, Budapest, and Paris, and even though they insisted on staying with me, they finally acquiesced to going home. Both of them had to return to work the next morning. (I have never used acquiesce in a sentence, yet it flowed right in, and I let it stay.)

On Christmas night, my new sister and I had stayed and waited for the tests to be completed. While I dozed, she occupied her time with her tablet and reminding me to breathe. This had nothing to do with the reason we were in the hospital, but because I tend to stop breathing when I sleep without my breathing machine. I found out later that prior to leaving, Shannan had told her to remind me to breathe since I was drowsy from the morphine.

At that point I had had a couple of intravenous doses of morphine and was feeling much less pain, at least enough so I could doze while still being aware of the noises in the busy unit, which included, as I learned later, my own alarm beeping as my oxygen level dropped. As for the nausea, some intravenous medications had taken care of that earlier, and I did not begin to throw up until after I had been instructed to go home, given a referral to a surgeon, and told to call my doctor in the morning. After getting dressed and not seeing any staff available, I left a basin of my stomach contents on the bedside stand and, holding tightly onto my new family member, proceeded to wobble through the waiting room and out to the car with a clean basin clutched tightly to my chest.

Nathan, it amazes me that my emergency room experience, although reminiscent of yours, did not cause me to compare it to the day you died. The first seven years you were gone, I avoided hospitals and even had some anxiety when driving by them. That changed when Shannan was thirteen and required a visit to the emergency room for stitches after a biking accident. I found myself in a hospital emergency room with your sister, and although uncomfortable, I didn't panic. Also, after many trips through Saint Louis since the day you left, I no longer cringe when I see the skyline of that city or relive the drive to the emergency room with you. What a blessing that is, although I still have sadness and at times tear up. Instead of thinking of the last time I saw you in crisis, I now am able to envision how it will be when we meet in the here-after.

Which brings us back to where this dialog began—a new relatedness, a family dinner party last evening, and a ladies' dinner party three days prior. I think about that party at the newly renovated house and how my new sister belonged in the empty chair at the table. I also wonder about the journeys of the other six amazing women and how each of our different paths brought us to the dinner table in a recently renovated house two days after Christmas in the year 2013.

Now I wish I had known three days ago what I now know about the subdued woman to my left at that dinner party. We had met the week before at another luncheon. I would have connected in a deeper way had I known that she also had lost a son and within the last year. In fact, four of the seven at the dinner table have lost a son, and the other three women have sons who are now traveling through some lostness of their own. Journeys and stories of journeys, each of us has her own tales to tell. I wonder what each of these women would care to share of their own journey and what words of wisdom they would have? What insights would such a book contain?

I was inspired just today with a title for a new book while lingering in a bookstore with the newlyweds. We had some extra time before taking your new brother-in-law to see the newly renovated home of my friend. As I walked around the bookstore, inspiration for a book title came to mind as a result of the side effects of the potions from the emergency room episode. Experiencing the need to distance myself from these bad effects, I walked on while texting my thoughts to my friend. I laughed aloud as I imagined her reaction if she were to read my text now, while she is out to lunch with a new acquaintance. "I thought of a title for a new book: 'Fart Then Move On'", not *"Vapors – An Incentive to Move Forward"*. The new title doesn't have quite the same impact, does it? Later I realized that I do not need a new book, just the one I have already been thinking about for the last few days, a book about seven women and their journeys that brought them to a dinner party on a Friday a couple of days after Christmas.

The Friday night dinner party was in honor of a widowed friend (me) who had retired to New Mexico the previous year and was in town for a bit. The dinner party celebrated this woman having survived as mother of the bride and also celebrated the marriage of her daughter to a wonderful man with a family who also had become family. A book about all of these women would surely include similar bits of wisdom, And so, begins my quest to learn the stories that these women might care to tell and the conventional wisdom they would share. I will let you know how this journal of stories turns out.

Love, Mom

Going Home to the Mountains

January 20, 2015
Cincinnati

Dear Nathan,

I have again been at Shannan's in Cincinnati for the holidays and am now sitting in the airport, waiting for my return flight home to New Mexico. For the past several weeks, a scene from a television show has become stuck in my mind and has highlighted a point of view that I wasn't aware I held. We had been watching an apocalyptic television series, *Falling Skies*, and made it into the third of four seasons. Your dad used to say that one of these days we would be able to watch shows and movies on demand, and he was right. The plot of the series involved an alien invasion that had decimated the majority of the world's population.

The series followed a small group of American survivors. The medic was a girl who had been in her freshman year of premed prior to the war. Encamped in an abandoned town after fleeing with the group from a metropolitan area, she found a neighborhood church in which to pray. Another girl in her late teens, now a scout for the resistance, scoffed, "You still have faith?" The medic responded, "Some have lost their faith, but my faith is stronger than ever." The scout said, "Next time you're on your knees praying, see if the big guy can get us an operational B-52 bomber loaded with nukes." And the medic replied, "I don't think that's how it works. I don't tell God what to do; I ask God what I can do for him." Disdainfully, the scout stalked off to join the other resistance fighters.

I was surprised at my knee-jerk reaction to this scene. I found myself identifying with the scout. "What good is God if he doesn't do what I know I need?" Until that moment, I would have vigorously denied that I endorsed this belief. But here I was like someone observing the sun rising in the east and setting in the west, yet misunderstanding the relationship between the two, believing it is the sun that is in orbit. The young medic's perspective, however, was that she revolved around something greater: someone to serve. Although she was young, the scout as a soldier should have had more understanding regarding authority. However, both the scout and I responded as if we were symbolically at the center of our spiritual lives and that the Son of God's path depended upon us. But only a god of my own making could I command, however ineffective this would be, since such a god would have no greater knowledge or power than its creator: me.

When my life was spiraling out of control, the day you left for eternity, I did not doubt God or his love. I clung to a true relationship, in spite of my world becoming suddenly alien. It's more in the mundane things of my life that I sometimes live as if I command God. Yet at the most tragic time, like the medic, I knew in my heart that God was central. How could this have been? How was it that during the worst, my faith was the strongest? As I ponder this aspect of my faith walk, I now realize that an event four weeks prior to your leaving had somehow influenced my perception of who is really responsible for life.

A month earlier, just before Mother's Day, I had been wheeled into the operating room sobbing for what was the loss of the child I carried within. I heaped guilt upon myself for somehow not having prevented the death of this little one. I had forgotten until writing this letter, the words of the nun sent to speak with me in the recovery room. In response to my guilt-laden grief, she said, "You are not that powerful." I can now appreciate the impact of her words when four weeks later you died before Father's Day. Sitting on a table over to the side watching you slip away, I knew deep down in my soul and without doubt, that the only one who had the ability to control an unborn child's future and now yours was a sovereign God.

I remember when you were in the first and second grade, many a night during bedtime prayers, you would pray for children who didn't have families, houses, or food, and also for a baby brother. I once said, "Nathan, even if you got a baby brother, do you know how old you would be before he got big enough to play?" You said, "Oh, but Mom, think of all the things I could teach him!" Then that day in the emergency room when you left for eternity, I watched you peeking around from behind Jesus, both of you glowing so bright, and I heard him say, "It's okay." I knew that it really was, and it still is okay. Not only was God taking you with him, but he also had answered your prayer. You have a little brother in heaven with whom you can enjoy your life in eternity because Jesus, the Son of God, *is* at the center of it all.

It is comforting to know that it is God who is stable and that we on earth really are the ones in orbit. He does not revolve around my limited knowledge, abilities, or desires. My future is not totally of my own making. God after all has a plan as stated by Jeremiah. "For I know the plans I have for you," declares the Lord, "plans to prosper you and not to harm you, plans to give you hope and a future. Then you will call on me and come and pray to me, and I will listen to you. You will seek me and find me when you seek me with all your heart"[79]. God plans beyond our earthly existence and into eternity. Although you are gone from us, I am comforted with the certainty that I will see you again.

"Brothers and sisters, we do not want you to be uninformed about those who sleep in death, so that you do not grieve like the rest of mankind, who have no hope. For we believe that Jesus died and arose again, and so we believe that God will bring with Jesus those who have fallen asleep in him"[80].

One of these days, when my days here are finished, you along with your little brother and your dad will be there to greet me as well. Until then I will enjoy my life to the fullest.

That was then in 2015 – Now in 2023

---

79 Jeremiah 29:11–13 NIV
80 1 Thessalonians 4:13–14 NIV

The nun was right. I did not have the power to prevent an unborn child's death or yours. I did not have the power or knowledge to heal you or raise you from the dead, even if you would have been willing to leave your Jesus and come back. And I was also right about a Sovereign God having the power to step in and change the present and thus our future.

What I was wrong about, Nathan, was forgetting, in my distress, several truths. I had implied that since God was responsible for life he must also be responsible for ... *death*. I had forgotten familiar verses such as our enemy, the "thief comes not, but to steal, to kill and to destroy: I am come that they might have life, and that they might have it more abundantly"[81]. I mistakenly placed the responsibility for your death squarely on Jesus's shoulders because He didn't heal you, instead of acknowledging our fallen world, our arch enemy and ourselves not walking in the roles Jesus made possible for us with His death and resurrection. In the book of Acts in the Bible, after Jesus ascended into heaven, on the Day of Pentecost in the Upper Room, the disciples received power from Holy Spirit, resulting in them functioning with signs and wonders, even raising the dead. So why do I only infrequently hear of such? Yet this same power is beginning to be experienced in a greater way around the world and here in this country as well. Yes, we are beginning to experience a greater walk in the authority Adam lost to Satan and that Jesus bought back for us with his sacrifice and resurrection.

---

81 John 10:10 NKJV

Why on that day in the Emergency Room, didn't God step in and change our lives dramatically by raising you from the dead? When he didn't, like the scout in the beginning of this journal entry, I could have metaphorically said to God, "You're the Big Guy. Send us an operational B-52 bomber loaded with nukes!"

But Nathan, that's essentially *what God did* do for us both back in 1983. He sent greater power than that of a B-52 bomber loaded with nukes! I was six months pregnant with you when I drove to church alone on that evening. I left home without my seatbelt buckled because it was stuck, saying to myself, 'Ahh, it'll be ok". Upon leaving church that evening, again I couldn't get the seatbelt unstuck. On the way home, a man from out of town driving a pickup truck, entered the same intersection as I, but from the opposite direction. Suddenly he decided that he needed to turn left, NOW! And he did – at 35-40 mph! Since I was entering the same intersection, I had a mere second or two to realize a T-bone was imminent. Yet God intervened. An external thought like a physical voice vibrated around me, totally engulfing the space inside the car. *"Keep your arms straight!" "Keep your arms straight!"* I focused on locking my elbows as I held tightly to the steering wheel. My Mustang was totaled, rendering the driver's door crushed and the passenger door needing pried open before I could be helped out of the car. At the hospital, Nathan, you were determined to be perfectly safe within my womb. And I only sustained slightly sore elbows and a sprained ankle from locking the brake pedal to the floor.

Then at fifteen months old, Nathan, you were diagnosed with cancer of a kidney. The night before surgery, the oncologist, along with the surgeon, stood on the other side of your crib discussing what, as parents, to expect. He leaned forward over you, looked me directly in the eye and said. "He will be on chemotherapy for at least eighteen months. That's longer than he's been alive." We had recently moved to Alabama, so I called our pastor in Cincinnati for prayer. I remember how comforting it was to hear him say to me. "Don't worry about having enough faith. Our job is to have faith and pray. Your job is to just be Nathan's mother." He took the heavy weight off our shoulders and he and the church back home carried it. The next morning after surgery, the surgeon in confusion reported that in spite of all the tests having confirmed cancer, that was not the case! The labs on the tumor engulfing the removed kidney showed it not to be cancer!

Praise the Lord! God showed up for us *twice* with more power than that of a bomber and nukes! Wait! Make that three times, Nathan! Because He enabled me to see you standing with Jesus in the Emergency Room on the way to your new life in heaven! I wonder how many more times in our lives, God had rescued or intervened with great power for us, and we weren't even aware of it.

As I said in my letter, *Enduring Peace*, in the Prologue of this *Mars* book, I have to continually focus on *what God did* instead of what *he did not do*. What I know is that God is loving and just. And I know that death came into the world as a result of Adam and Eve's sin in the garden. God the Father sent Jesus Christ the Son of God to die so that we can live. Instead of scoffing in disdain like the scout in *Falling Skies*, I, like the medic "Ask what I can do for him." Publishing my and Nathan's story is one of the things that Holy Spirit has asked me to do for the Father.

In the hospital emergency room your last day here below, *what God did*, Nathan, was enable me to see your initial moments with Jesus. And as Jesus looked directly into my eyes, I could see and hear him clearly. "It's ok" heard not only in words, but in supernatural peace as well. Someday, we on earth will no longer be living under an alien invasion for *God's Kingdom will come on earth as it is in Heaven*. Surely, Jesus wouldn't have told the disciples to pray something that could never be. Jesus, instructed us, "This then is how you should pray"[82].

> Our Father which art in heaven,
> Hallowed be thy name.
> *Thy kingdom come,*
> *Thy will be done in earth,*
> *as it is in heaven.*
> Give us this day our daily bread.
> And forgive us our debts,
> as we forgive our debtors.
> And lead us not into temptation,
> but deliver us from evil:
> For thine is the kingdom, and the power,
> and the glory, forever. Amen"[83].

One day when my work is done here on earth, I will see both you and Jesus again with more clarity than I did when Jesus came into a little boy's emergency room to take him home to heaven. I will see clearly because I will be in the light *with* you. Yes, I'll be bathed

---

82 Mathew 6:9 NIV
83 Matthew 6:9-13 KJV

in the light of His glory and submersed in incredible peace that so far passes understanding that it is impossible to fully describe. For now, I will continue to dwell on what God has done for me and also for you. And I will focus on what he is doing today and will do each day until I am reunited with you, your dad and little brother.

We did a bit of time travel there to 2023. Now we will return to where we left off in 2015.

Love, Mom

We're a Team

February 17, 2015
Sacramento Mountains, NM

Dear Nathan,

I was just sitting here thinking about our first Thanksgiving without you. It was also your first birthday away from us. I frequently listen to the echoes of my memory of that morning, with your voice whispering to my heart.

> *Mom, remember when I could travel so fast on my bike, with the wind whistling through my hair?*
>
> *Now I can think myself to Mars.*

Your last year here, my cousin Nita came to stay with us until she found a job and a place of her own in Cincinnati after moving from Texas. On several occasions, I heard her say to you during your discussions, "Nathan, you are just too deep for someone your age!"

Unknown to me at the time of our trip to Saint Louis, you had been told a few days earlier of your friend's dream that you died in a faraway place. However, by the end of our road trip you focused on what awaited you on the other side instead of your possible death here below. King Solomon said that God "has made everything beautiful in its time. He has also set eternity in the hearts of men; yet no one can fathom what God has done from the beginning to end"[84].

Memories of you and your all-too-brief time here on earth leave a trail through my mind. I remember your exuberance for life and yet your focus on eternity, reminding me of your father's poem "I Hear Nathan," written when you were a baby. And as he said then, I say now, "I will attend to your insistent plea" or as I imagined it to be in *A Son's Final Goodbye*.

> *Tell them I'm in heaven with Jesus,*
> *Tell them how to get here*

Yes, we're a team, Nathan; we're a team; we will tell them, you and I. We *will* tell them.

Love, Mom

---

[84] Ecclesiastes 3:11 NIV

A Walk of Grace

Summer 2015

We've now come to the end of the chronicle of my journey of walking in faith since Nathan's passing on to his forever life. As you have read my story, you have become aware of my interpretation of the names of my immediate family:

Nathan Oliver Walker—
 One Who Walks in God's Gift of Peace
Shannan Hope Walker—
 Wise One Who Walks in Hope
Richard Thomas Walker—
 One Who Walks and Leads with the
 Strength of Twins

Now I would like to share how I understand the meaning of my own name, which I appreciate in a different light than I did as a child. My parents, although not perfect, did the most important thing: they raised me in the knowledge of the Lord. Shortly after Nathan passed away, Mom called to say that she had just learned what my middle name meant. She apologized and said that she would understand if I chose to no longer use the name Dolores. In grade school I used to wonder why my parents would name me "extreme sorrow and pain." When I married, I took the opportunity to replace Dolores with my maiden name. However, if I had kept my middle name, I would now be –

Grace Dolores Walker—
 One Who Walks in the Mercy and Favor
 of the Lord Amid Great Sorrow

How apt, for it is indeed the Lord's mercy and favor that has allowed me to walk my walk of faith, and to not only endure but to also flourish.

Thank you for reading this book and experiencing that journey with me. I hope I have shown just how much my everlasting bond with Nathan and my unequivocal trust in God provided the sustenance that fortified and inspired me to go on. When Holy Spirit nurtures and sustains us, we have truly discovered what life is about, for that spirit-level nourishment is the essence of both faith and love.

And so, having traveled my own path, I encourage you as you travel yours. Whoever you are and wherever you are on your own walk, I honor your courage and strength, and I empathize with you, for every true spiritual odyssey entails some form of struggle.

It is my hope that sharing my story with you has given you the inspiration, solace, and encouragement to keep walking. For as scripture says, "Praise be to the God and Father of our Lord Jesus Christ, the Father of compassion and the God of all comfort, who comforts us in all our troubles, so that we can comfort those in any trouble with the comfort we ourselves have received from God"[85]. I bless you as God instructed Moses to teach a blessing over the people.

> "The Lord bless you and keep you;
> the Lord make his face shine on you
> and be gracious to you;
> the Lord turn his face toward you
> and give you peace"[86].

Grace Hournbuckle Walker

---

[85] 2 Corinthians 1:3–4 NIV

[86] Numbers 6:24–26 NIV Priestly Blessing God gave Moses for the Priests Arron and sons to bless the people.

Epilogue

2015-2023

Epilogue contains poems and essays written as I processed the possible results of spilling my guts to the world by having published such a personal story as my 2016 edition of this, Nathan's *Mars* book. This section also reflects my current quest to identify Father God's purpose and assignments for me going forward as it relates to His Kingdom here on earth.

Erbal Tease

Late October 2015

Now that the *Mars* book is in the publication process, I am enjoying the early morning hour without a deadline to meet. A great cup of coffee sitting on the windowsill, I'm thinking that if I knew what is good for me, I would change my usual morning drink to herbal teas. However, in my mind's eye, I see "e-r-b-a-l and t-e-a-s-e". Intrigued with speaking this phrase softly into the room at large, I decide to see where this verbal concoction is taking me. So, pulling out my computer, I type "e-r-b-a-l" and am promptly encouraged to replace this, my chosen word, with "h-e-r-b-a-l". However, my computer is quickly satisfied when I choose another option; "add to dictionary"! If only all improvements in my life were this easy.

As I gaze out the window this morning, I continue to ponder the impact of spoken words, useful phrases and life choices. So, come along with me this drizzly fall morning in the Midwest. Think: "cloudy, semi-dark with tall trees still and leaveless". My computer recommends "sleeveless", while mid-level honeysuckle wave gently at me still covered in foliage. Bushes covered in foliage, not me. And yep, I did just add "leaveless" to my dictionary. However, I must insist on being given credit for correcting the spelling of foliage instead of adding "f-o-i-l-a-g-e" to my dictionary.

My mom used to tell us kids that we couldn't use a word if it wasn't in the dictionary. That is, she was adamant about this, until we found our favorite example, "ain't" documented for all to see. Which, I must say, my computer is not acquainted with…. hum… maybe I should just add that as well! There! Now "ain't" is officially a word available for one of life's many choices! Use it freely! Ain't, a word that I'm sure we have all made use of despite our elders' dutiful admonishment against the practice.

Now that I think about it, there are many words common to our family dialogue, which were not in my school's dictionary. For example, "row-snears", my grandfather's favorite food, is an example of a word or phrase that made more sense after I learned to read. I found it spelled "roasting ears" once in a book! Imagine that! Reading sheds a lot of light! "Chester drawers": I always wondered why my brother had a piece of furniture named after him. Must admit that I was jealous of his prestige. And yes, I also learned the truth about that one from reading.

In spite of incorrect spelling or mispronounciation[87], these words were heartily approved by the guardians of our family dialect. Upon double checking the spelling of "pronounciation" I read that this word from the 14th century was replaced with 15th century "pronunciation". This latter word became the standard in 1610 due to changes in definition of both words over the centuries.

---

87 Pronounciation Vs Pronunciation, Which One Should You Use? (thecontentauthority.com)

"Pronounciation" is now officially labeled "nonexistent". I didn't realize we were such an "Old Family", but we must be if our vocabulary contains a 14th century word which is now considered extinct! Yet, how can a word be extinct and still be "alive and well" in a portion of the populace's vocabulary? Since we are now noted to be Old Family, wonder if this means we are also "Old Money"? That would certainly come in handy!

Words misunderstood until viewed upon the printed page, reminds me of questionable songs of my youth. Ever wonder about the wording of some of the gospel songs from our childhood? Singing along fervently in congregational worship, I pondered why some words, although alright in church, were not allowed in everyday conversation. Why would a word sang on Sunday morning be met with such strong disapproval when used in conversation with my brothers? Whether in anger or while *"conversing softly and lovingly"*, the use of this word could have been met with the threat of having my mouth washed out with soap! Coming readily to mind is the song; "Oh Hail, King Jesus". Sound familiar? Now what do you think, prior to me learning to read, I thought we were singing? If you still have not a clue, say the song title again in a modified Texas drawl common in Southeastern New Mexico.

Do you suppose the congregation was bemoaning our ordinary and sometimes very difficult lives or were they greeting the King of the universe? Yep, sure was surprised by that one upon learning to read. Now that I can read The Book for myself, do I still sing a song of lament? Or am I now able to understand enough of Jesus' story to allow myself to sing a joyful greeting? Would I believe the story, if I had no prior knowledge, but were to hear about Jesus right now for the first time? How would I at this moment understand the details of his story? To what extent would I allow this new information to affect me? Would this story make a significant difference to me or in how I live my life? Would I embrace the story today if I had just heard about an infant and a kingdom which was said to come?

Just imagine for a moment, if what is said about Jesus as the eternal king were true! Would I hear it right, or would the truth I hear be censored by the person I am? Would I, who live the driven life of the American in a dream, understand the story or would I be influenced by my culture's dialect and beliefs? Is it possible for me to grasp the significance of the story of King Jesus and to fully understand that the light is meant to focus not on me or my life, but to fully illuminate the eternal story?

Today, this is how I hear and understand the story.

Eternal Being ... Earth created
　Adam and Eve disobeyed... Lost from Paradise[88]
　　Ruled by fallen angel... Evil reigns
　　　Man needs help... Back to Eden
　　　　Enter baby ... Human yet Eternal Being
　　　　　Crucified & Resurrected ... Authority recovered
　　　　　　Acceptance... Way back to Paradise[89]

The light of learning provides illumination for a more complete understanding; row-snears and roasting ears, Chester drawers

---

[88] Paradise - Place with Presence of God, Genesis 2:8 Garden of Eden, Not used here for Sheol, holding place for righteous dead before Christ's death and resurrection

[89] 2 Corinthians 12:2-4 Paradise, 3rd Heaven, Revelation 21 and 22 City of Light, Holy City, New Jerusalem coming down from Heaven

and chest of drawers, hell or hail. Understanding can enlighten truth and distinguish differences in perception. It all comes down to knowing and experiencing. The corn tastes just as sweet, the storage is just as useful no matter how it is that we first heard or understood. I know now that just because it is not in my dictionary or in The Book, in the way that I heard or was told to me; doesn't mean that the essence or truth is not present. How much light is required for the brightness of truth to illuminate my understanding of the King? Do I continue to bemoan my life, or can I now fully accept the light that focuses on the complete story of eternity and so, joyfully sing "Oh, Hail, King Jesus"!

Incognito versus Assimilation

February 2016

Incognito – having identity concealed.

Assimilation – process by which social and psychological characteristics of a group are acquired.

This morning I was reviewing my computer file of photos, looking for a specific one I had taken a couple of years ago when I lived in hot semi-arid Carlsbad, New Mexico. I searched for a picture of a horned toad taken on an early summer morning. The toad had been sitting among the small leafy green plants growing against the foundation of the well house[90]. I planned to print the photo with name and date. His name from our childhood would certainly never do. In our innocence of not only linguistics and grammar but also of life, we would have called him a "horny toe".

However, this morning, while considering a portrait title, I pondered what the toad may have been thinking as he stilled, waiting for the click of the shutter. "Maybe she will think I belong

---

[90] Well house. Small building housing pump for water well sometimes referred to as pump house.

here. I look a lot like the concrete." "Maybe she won't see me. After all, I blend in with the twigs and branches beneath these small leaves. No worries." "Uh oh! I think she's spotted me! But I don't think I can successfully make a break for it." Thus, confronted by his inability to remain incognito, was the toad really considering his options? Hide, run or stand my ground? Or perhaps he was thinking something else entirely. "Sure is nice and cool in the damp from the dripping faucet. Maybe I could make myself at home here by the well house foundation instead of in the hot sand beneath the cactus across the yard."

Sometimes the place in which I find myself is so unlike what I grew up with that, like the toad, I try to conceal who I really am. My first book is to be released soon. Now that is definitely the epitome of incognito: twenty-five years writing a book and hiding my true ambition. Now what am I going to do? What happens next? I consider my options. Maybe I am so blended into my life with family, friends and church community that I should just continue in this quite retired life. Surely after my book *Now I Can Think Myself to Mars* is published, no one will expect another one, will they? No worries. No expectations of a Grandma Moses[91] spark of creativity from me at this point in my life, a life of hiding. Or I could strive to conform to the social or psychological characteristics of "author" to define who I am. Once I learn what that is, of course. But wouldn't that also be hiding?

---

[91] Grandma Moses - Anna Mary Robertson Moses 1860-1961. A self-taught artist who began painting at 78 years of age when she became unable to do needlework and quilt pictures of farm life due to arthritis. A New York collector, Louis J. Caldor saw her work and helped her begin exhibiting internationally into her 90s and painted until a few months before her death at age 101. National Museum of Women the Arts

I might be able to return to the Sacramento Mountains in New Mexico and resume helping my brothers work on our properties. I shouldn't have a problem re-acclimating to the 8-10,000 feet altitude. Or I could just stay halfway down the "hill" yet still overlooking the basin. I do like cactus and red cliffs crowned with wide blue skies overlooking an incredible view of the basin with its beautiful White Sands[92] and the mountain ranges beyond. I'd keep busy enough and there wouldn't be any pressure to pursue writing. Did someone just say "Run"?

However, like the toad enjoying the newness of a refreshing place alongside the well house, maybe I too can stand my ground. I can become comfortable in a wonderful and exciting new environment, that of being an author. I already have a title for a new book which is still in draft form. And of course my geographical location needn't interfere with my new career as long as I don't get so involved in other stuff that I end up hiding or running instead of making a stand.

As I began writing this piece, I thought it would be a discussion of the choice which confronts a novice Christ Follower: living incognito in immaturity versus assimilating into a mature life made possible by the Creator. Yet, as mentioned above, I find myself identifying with the toad in a different manner. And although I have had a lifelong journey with Christ, sometimes following him with more success than at other times, I now find myself in an entirely foreign place in my walk. This new yet excitingly strange

---

[92] https://www.nps.gov/whsa/ White Sands National Park. Rising from the heart of the Tularosa Basin is one of the world's great natural wonders - the glistening **white sands** of **New Mexico**.

place is that of a writer, and yes, otherwise known as a retiree. I like where I currently find myself. However, being a toad, can I survive with my inherent characteristics intact and still foster the peace, growth and creativity of assimilation into this new career?

Yes! I choose to stand my ground and assimilate into this new role. The process for me now consists not only of exercising my writing muscles, but also of learning from experienced authors. I foresee seminars, webinars, newsletters and editors becoming more prominent in my life. Even so, I must first of all remember that the strongest source of reliability is my Creator. The psalmist said, "Teach me knowledge and good judgment for I trust your commands..."[93]. And the wisest of all men, Solomon, gave this advice, "The fear *(reverence, awe and worship)* of the LORD is the beginning of knowledge but fools despise wisdom and instruction"[94]. Keeping God in the equation, including reverent awe and worship, will allow my identity to be tempered, not eclipsed by knowledge and experience. As the Psalmist said, "For you (*Lord, God*) created my inmost being; you knit me together in my mother's womb. I praise you because I am fearfully and wonderfully made; your works are wonderful; I know that full well"[95].

Now, like the novice Christ Follower, if I embrace learning, I will be able to increase in maturity. No longer being incognito, I choose to neither hide nor run. My goal is to stand my ground, allowing assimilation into this, my new role, without losing the uniqueness placed within me by my Creator. And like the toad enjoying the

---

93 Psalm 119:66 NIV
94 Proverbs 1:7 NIV
95 Psalm 139:13-14 NIV

cool refreshing spot by the well house, I'll stand my ground and see how it goes.

Inspiration for "Lament of a Tarnished Vessel"

September 8, 2016

The 1st edition of *Now I Can Think Myself to Mars* had just been published summer 2016. I was feeling trepidation due to having spilled my guts to the world by publishing such a very personal book. What would be the public's response? What will people think of Nathan's and my stories? Had I written too much? Had I shared enough? What impact will the book have on those who haven't lost children but have other major losses and challenges? Would what I said help those suffering great loss of their own?

Somehow I must *Get Ready* for whatever the response to both me and my book. Then I realized the greatest thing to pay attention to was the approval I felt from Father God of me, Nathan's story and the book as a whole. I realize that I am not the only one that has felt they don't measure up or are not prepared for the challenges ahead. That's the problem with measuring ourselves against others instead of listening to the Master calling to us personally. I trust you find *Lament of a Tarnished Vessel* inspiring more confidence in him that you can do what he has set in your heart to do. And that you will be doing it, not alone, but with the Master's guidance and inspiration.

Lament of a Tarnished Vessel

September 8, 2016

Get Ready

Hearing frantic disgorging of cupboards
Dispersing flour, oil, salt across counters
Gathering of vessels by experienced hands
Chopping, baking, roasting in advance of a great event

Oh, how I hope it all continues to flow
In purposeful intent without me
Love and perfection swirling around me
Leaving me untouched

Cringing further into the darkness of the butler pantry
Purposeful steps advancing as I knew they would
For I have seen the commotion of preparation before
A feast, an anticipation of celebration

Knowing expectations... theirs... mine
Only the best, the most worthy of vessels
Hiding, I find myself preventing their perceptions
Their disappointment at my appearance

Get Ready!

I glance forward as sudden illumination
Beyond the opening door
Strikes the choicest ones
On the most prominent shelf

Gleaming in favor, polished in love
Experienced in service,
Tea Set straightens in expectation
I shrink within myself for tarnish is upon me

Praying for the closing of the door
Leaving me in obscurity
Fearing the disappointment of the Master
The ridiculing of the others

Then... a strong voice of Love,
"Where is it? My Father gave it me
For just this purpose, no other will do
Quick, bring it out into the light!"

Get Ready!

"Oh, just see the detail
forged into this vessel by my Father
He made it with his own hands
In perfection!"

Me? You want me?
But I have been unable to remove the tarnish
Please don't bring me out of my dark corner
For unworthiness is upon me

Not gleaming as do the others
Master deserving of more, of the best
Only those experienced and
Polished for service

Again the Master's voice, "I must have it!
My Father created it in Love for just this purpose
I will polish it myself into the beauty
Crafted by my Father for service, for celebration!"

Remember the Potter

August 30, 2017

I awoke one morning this summer imagining two pots having a conversation while sitting on a shelf in a Village Shop window.

- *One pot says meekly to the other –*

"You seem so proud of where you are."

"Why, of course, I am," answers the other pot. "I've accomplished a lot to be who and what I am. Look at the detail and brilliant colors with which I am adorned. And it's not every pot that exhibits such a fine shape. But just look at yourself. Don't you wish you could be like me, especially since you have that crack running across you and halfway up your side?"

Meek Pot responds, "Do you remember the beginning?"

"What do you mean, the beginning? I've always been right here," says Proud Pot.

"Don't you remember being a lump of clay, spinning round and round on the Potter's wheel?" Meek Pot questions persistently.

"Remember the feel of water dripping down your sides as the Potter's hands formed you? Can't you remember how your world spun seemingly out of control? Don't you remember the fire, the intense fire hardening you to the shape that you are now? Or the glazing of the beautiful colors chosen for you? Or can you remember being placed carefully here on this shelf in front of the window?"

Meek Pot continues, "You are right that I was damaged. And like you, I didn't used to remember the beginning… until I was broken. Then I felt the Potter's hands tenderly gathering me up, repairing my cracks and restoring my memories of the beginning. Then he sat me here on the shelf beside you."

"Don't you remember?"

- *Voice of shopkeeper to customer –*

"Here's the pot … Oh, no. No, honey. No, ma'am. Don't choose that pot!'

"It does look pretty and looks great on the shelf, but it won't be very useful. Now, notice this pot beside that one. This slightly smaller one is the pot for you."

Lady customer, "But that one has a crack."

"You're right, it does have a crack. However, because of the craftsmanship of the creator and his restoration, the crack is the strongest, most beautiful part of the pot," explains Shopkeeper.

"It's like a lightning bolt of vivid color, don't you agree? Besides, this smaller pot contains a healing salve."

"That pot may look like it's a better pot, but it's empty. It's not going to be of much use to you unless you just want to sit and look at it. But if you want something that is going to bless you and have an impact on your life, then you need this one."

Shopkeeper, picking up the smaller pot and turning it slightly, continues his explanation.

"Ma'am look closely while I turn the pot just a little bit toward the light. There, can you see something else within the colors glazed into the pot? If you look carefully, you will see a reflection of the Creator, for His likeness has been fired into this pot while restoring it".

"This is the pot for you. It contains restorative power for cleansing and healing. Yes, this small pot has been restored, more beautiful than before and filled with *The Balm of Gilead*!"[96] [97]

---

[96] Genesis 37:25, Jeremiah 8:21-22, 46:11

[97] GotQuestions.org – High quality aromatic medicinal ointment with healing properties from Gilead, an area east of the Jordan River.

Survival in the Deserts of Life

February 2018

A few years ago in New Mexico, I had taken a wrong turn in the desert. That was bad enough, but then a 'ding', and a warning light on the dash signaled that my truck had gone as far as it would go. I wrote about this event previously in Part II of this book in *What Did You Go Out to the Desert to See?* September 28, 2012. I was proud that I had followed my mother's instructions for survival while growing up in the Southwest. As I pondered life's lessons from that day's little jaunt into the desert, I saw several productive directions. I could discuss being equipped for spiritual survival. Or I could even discuss how giving myself permission to see beauty, although not removing the trial, allows me to survive without despair. However, the phrase that kept going through my mind at that time was a question Jesus had asked the crowd concerning John the Baptist. "What did you go out to the desert to see?"

Now here I am, back to discuss the first topic I considered back then, that of tools for *Spiritual Survival* in the deserts of life: *Forgiveness, Bread of life, Sword of the Spirit and Emergency Plan for your Ever-After.*

Forgiveness - of all wrongdoing; those of mine and others against me, for *all* have sinned.[98] Sin is defined as breaking any of the commandments of God at any time. No one has ever been perfect since the fall of mankind in the Garden of Eden bringing sin into our world. Therefore we as flawed individuals satisfy ourselves if we avoid being guilty of what we view as the worst offences. How can God possibly expect perfect compliance?

One of the teachers of the law asked Jesus, "Of all the commandments, which is the most important?" Jesus responded by quoting from Deuteronomy and Leviticus in the Old Testament[99].

'The most important one,' answered Jesus, "is this:
'Hear O Israel:
The Lord our God, the Lord is one.
Love the Lord your God
with all your heart and
with all your soul and
with all your mind and
with all your strength.'

The second is this:
'Love your neighbor as yourself.'

There is no commandment greater than these"[100].

---

98 Romans 3:23 NIV
99 Deuteronomy 6:4-5 and Leviticus 19:18
100 Mark 12:28-31 NIV

I'm sure we all realize that fulfilling the Two Love Commandments Jesus described, is just as or even more impossible than keeping the Ten Commandments given Moses in the desert for the Children of Israel. In the Garden of Eden, Adam and Eve failed to keep even the One Commandment given them. But God had a plan. When asked by his followers how they should pray, Jesus taught them what we refer to as "The Lord's Prayer". I discussed this in *Going Home to the Mountains* letter January 20, 2015. Jesus, when teaching prayer made two statements we didn't learn as children reciting "The Lord's Prayer". These two qualifiers are crucial to understand regarding the portion from the prayer "And forgive us our debts, as we forgive our debtors"[101]. After the prayer, Jesus then said,

> "For if ye forgive men their trespasses,
> your heavenly Father will also forgive you:
> But if ye forgive not men their trespasses,
> Neither will your Father forgive your trespasses"[102].

Debts and trespasses are wrongs committed against another. We must ask for or extend forgiveness whether or not it is asked of us. Situations are very different. It may not be appropriate or even possible to speak to another regarding a trespass. However, it is our responsibility to pardon others or sometimes even ourselves to prevent inflicting our hearts with bitterness.

---

[101] Mathew 6:12 KJV
[102] Matthew 6:14-15 KJV

I recently realized that although I had released a degree of resentment for a trespass committed against one of my ancestors and the family, I had not yet fully forgiven this grievous wrong. Sometimes Holy Spirit will prompt us to deal with something we don't realize we are still holding onto. I was then required to completely release my family's debtor, and all lingering animosity. A lifestyle of forgiveness is crucial in our relationship with God the Father as taught by Jesus the Christ.

This also requires us to repent which means to go in a different direction. Jesus said "Neither do I condemn you. Go and sin no more."[103]

Bread of life – Jesus is the manna from heaven, saying "I am the living bread that came down from heaven"[104]. As the manna sustained Moses and the children in the desert, so Jesus sustains our spirits and feeds our souls. The crowds looked for Jesus after he had fed 5,000 and he told them that instead of looking for him because "'you ate the loaves and had your fill, do not work for food that spoils, but for food that endures to eternal life, which the Son of Man will give you. For on him God the Father has placed his seal of approval.' Then they asked him, 'What must we do to do the work God requires?' Jesus answered, 'The work of God is this: to believe in the one he has sent'"[105].

When the Apostle Paul and Steven were released from prison by angels, the keeper of the prison asked "Sirs, what must I do to be

---

103 John 8:11
104 John 6:51a KJV
105 John 6:26- NIV

saved? And they said, Believe on the Lord Jesus Christ, and thou shalt be saved, and thy house"[106].

Sword of the Spirit – The Bible teaches us to be strong in the Lord, putting on the full armor of God. The full armor includes the belt of truth, breastplate of righteousness, feet shod with gospel of peace, shield of faith, helmet of salvation, and the sword of the Spirit. Then we can take our stand against the devil's schemes. Our struggle is not against flesh and blood... so when days of evil come, we can firmly stand our ground... using the "Sword of the Spirit which is the Word of God"[107]. This is speaking, declaring and decreeing God's Word concerning any situation.

Emergency plan for your Ever-After-Life – "If you confess with your mouth that Jesus is Lord and believe in your heart that God raised him from the dead, you will be saved"[108]. *If you have never confessed and believed this Bible verse, then I suggest you consider doing so now, as your emergency plan for spiritual survival.* I know many of you out there just bristled up at that phrase. You sat back further into your chair to distance yourself from such a thought and with a huff said aloud; "You can't expect to live anyway you want, then with your last breath, ask God to forgive you and take you to heaven!" Others of you probably have said this about yourself as well. However, if that is where you are at this moment, reach out and pull the rip cord, call out to God before you plummet to your eternal torment in death with a lifesaving parachute safely folded

---

106 Acts 16:30-31 KJV
107 Ephesians 6:10-18 NIV
108 Romans 10:9 NKJV

behind you. Scripture says in Romans, "For 'whoever calls on the name of the Lord shall be saved'"[109].

The thief on the cross seized just such an opportune moment, one of his last, to make a final request. "'Lord, remember me when You come into Your kingdom' and Jesus said to him, "Assuredly, I say to you, today you will be with Me in paradise"[110] There was no berating the thief for waiting till his imminent death. I don't advise those of you not on your last breath to wait till the end though, for suddenly that moment may be upon you so fast that before you realize it is coming, it is already gone.

Living for God is a safe bet, not necessarily for a trouble-free life, as evidenced by living in a fallen world. I discussed this aspect of life in detail in the January 20, 2015 journal entry – *Going Home to the Mountains*. Living for God is, however, a safe bet for comfort and guidance from God in life here below, followed by forever life with our Creator and Savior – Guaranteed by the death and resurrection of the Christ, the Son of God.

I implore you to allow yourself to follow not only the guidelines for survival in the desert as taught by my mother, but also to put into action God's rules for spiritual survival. "For 'I know the plans I have for you,' declares the Lord, 'plans to prosper you and not to harm you, plans to give you hope and a future'"[111]. This is God's nature, to plan not just for the children of Israel, but for all of us as well. The evidence is written all throughout his Word, culminating

---

[109] Romans 10:13 NKJV
[110] Luke 23: 42-43 NKJV
[111] Jeremiah 29:11 NIV

in the New Testament. Be blessed and consider God's plans to prosper you, give you hope and a future.

Inspiration for the Poem "Bedtime Prayer of a Warrior King"

July 27, 2022

This poem is based on my own bedtime prayer and Father God's answer. Last night imagining myself a child curled up in Father God's lap. I was just resting in His presence.

I expressed my desire to fulfill the destiny created for me. "For we are God's handiwork, created in Christ Jesus to do good works, which God prepared in advance for us to do."[112] While drifting off to sleep, I asked Him to teach me more about our relationship.

Father God's answer to my own bedtime prayer that night, resulted in me being awakened twice. Each time I saw a vision of myself before Father God on His throne. I stood as a man, understanding this to represent man in the generic sense – mankind. I also understood that I represented those who are "... in Christ Jesus you are all children of God through faith"[113].

---

112 Ephesians 2:10 NIV
113 Galatians 3:26 NIV

In the first vision I saw myself a young man in the uniform of a Priestly[114] Prince of the realm. I knew I was experienced in service within the Kingdom and expecting an expansion of my duties. I then fell quickly back to sleep.

Awakened again and saw a vision of myself older, more mature, stronger with higher rank and medals on my uniform. Standing with greater confidence and authority, I was a Conquering Warrior[115] King[116] reporting to Father God. Again, I fell quickly back to sleep.

Awakening the morning following and remembering the bedtime prayer I was taught as a child:

> *Now I lay me down to sleep*
> *I pray the Lord my soul to keep*
> *If I die before I wake*
> *I pray the Lord my soul to take* [117]

I then penned … *Bedtime Prayer of a Warrior King*.

> In this poem, I am using the Covenant name of God, "Yahweh"[118] which is the sound of breathing, to denote reverential deep breaths of sleep between stanzas. Breathe in with the first syllable then out with the second.

    Y a h – w e h … Y a h – w e h … Y a h – w e h

---

114 1 Peter 2:9 re royal priesthood
115 Ephesians 6:10-18 re fighting with spiritual armor to stand against devils schemes not against flesh and blood
116 1 Timothy 6:12 …fight good fight of faith… , Revelations 1:5-6, 5:10 re made us kings and priests before God
117 *Now I lay me down to sleep*. https://www.commonprayers.org/now-i-lay-me-down-to-sleep Prayer first printed in Thomas Fleet's "New England Primer" in year 1737.
118 https://www.gotquestions.org/breathe-Yahweh.html

Bedtime Prayer Of a Warrior King

The song adaptation of this poem, produced by
Observations Of Grace Music, is available at
www.youtube.com/@observationsofGrace

July 27, 2022

As I lay me down to sleep
Child curled, Father God, in your keep
Where you're sitting upon your throne
I crave relationship yet known

If I die before I wake
I pray my purpose not forsake
My destiny from creation
To complete duties my mission

Christ has made conceivable
Father's adoption possible[119]
With Jesus spiritually sit[120]
To you, Abba Father, submit[121]

Yahweh ... Yahweh ... Yahweh

---

119 Ephesians 1:5-14, Romans 8:14-17
120 Ephesians 2:5-7
121 Galatians 4:6, 1 Corinthians 15:26-27

Waken night, myself grown
Priestly Prince standing before throne
Thanksgiving and Praise my mantle
Intercessor, Shining Candle[122]

Yahweh... Yahweh... Yahweh

Awoke a Conquering King
True to Holy Spirit's leading
For next Kingdom duty to trod
Warrior[123] King before Father God

Yahweh... Yahweh... Yahweh

With both my mantles[124] and sword[125]
Powerful with Christ Jesus, Lord
Fully equipped with armor[126] on
Strong Faith wields Sword of Spirit drawn

---

122 Matthew 5:14-16 You are the light of the world... let your light shine before others, that they may see your good deeds and glorify your Father in heaven.

123 Ephesians 6:10-18 ...be strong in Lord and power of his might... we wrestle not against flesh and blood...

124 Mantle - Encyclopedia of The Bible - Bible Gateway 2nd priestly mantle 3rd type mantle of kings and especially of prophets.

125 Ephesians 6:17-18 sword of Spirit which is the Word of God. Prayers and supplications in the Spirit.

126 Ephesians 6:10-18 whole armor of God; truth, righteousness, gospel of peace, faith, salvation.

When I lay me down to sleep
Warrior King in Father God's keep
Intention certain from your throne
Kings and Priests before you, now known

If I die before I wake
I decree my purpose not brake[127]
My destiny from creation
Designed for your Kingdom Mission

Now I lay me down to sleep
Curled, Daddy God, into your keep
And say your purpose from the throne
Forever I'm your very own

Y a h w e h ... Y a h w e h ... Y a h w e h

Note – Final stanza written suitable for Child's Bedtime Prayer.

---

127 Merriam Webster. Transitive verb – to slow or stop as if by a brake.

Blessings and Comfort

June 4, 2023

Thank you for reading *Now I Can Think Myself To Mars* which is not only my eight-year-old son's adventures here below and his final goodbye. It is the story of this mother's renewal after loss of a child and the continual refreshing of my life in Christ over thirty years since Nathan's final goodbye in 1992. It's the eternal story. It is the ultimate invitation to embark now on an adventure which begins "If you declare with your mouth, 'Jesus is Lord,' and believe in your heart that God raised him from the dead, you will be saved"[128]. It is a life that continues on after the believer passes from mortality … and steps into immortality with God the Eternal three in One: Father, Son and Holy Spirit…

At the beginning of Jesus's ministry he called Simon Peter, a fisherman, to follow him and become a "fisher of men". Then late in his life, as an apostle, Peter wrote to the Christians in Rome. A portion of that letter is translated in The Message Bible as follows:

---

128 Romans 10:9 NIV

"Everything that goes into a life of pleasing God has been miraculously given to us by getting to know, personally and intimately, the One who invited us to God. The best invitation we ever received! We were also given absolutely terrific promises to pass on to you – your tickets to participation in the life of God after you turned your back on a world corrupted by lust. So don't lose a minute in building on what you've been given, complementing your basic faith with good character, spiritual understanding, alert discipline, passionate patience, reverent wonder, warm friendliness, and generous love, each dimension fitting into and developing the others. With these qualities active and growing in your lives, no grass will grow under your feet, no day will pass without its reward as you mature in your experience of our Master Jesus. Without these qualities you can't see what's right before you, oblivious that your old sinful life has been wiped off the books. So, friends, confirm God's invitation to you, his choice of you. Don't put it off: do it now"[129].

The Gospel of John records "For God so loved the world, that he gave his only begotten Son, that whosoever believeth in him should not perish, but have everlasting life"[130].

---

[129] 2 Peter 1:3-10 MSG
[130] John 3:16 KJV

Thank you for reading this *Mars* book. May you be blessed with more than endurance for earthly ups and downs. May you also experience fully all the blessings and joy available in our Lord Jesus Christ. I pray you take the opportunity if you haven't already, to experience the love of God the Father, Jesus Christ the Son and Holy Spirit our Helper and Comforter here below.

Be Blessed and Comforted by the
Three in One who loves you best

Grace Hournbuckle Walker

Author Interviews

2016 Book Trailer - YouTube
Now I Can Think Myself to Mars by Grace Hournbuckle Walker – 60 sec – YouTube

2022 January – Radio interview with Susan Sherayko https://soundcloud.com/user-320675991/grace-walker-in-rebuilding-your-life-radio-with-susan-sherayko

2023 February 18 – Author Interview PWWN TV – Preach the Word Worldwide Network – BOOKS OF THE MONTH SHOW – Playing: BOTM w 2-18-23 w Grace Hournbuckle Walker and Susan Gitelson.mp4 (ptwwnuploads.net)

www.ingramcontent.com/pod-product-compliance
Lightning Source LLC
LaVergne TN
LVHW010158070526
838199LV00062B/4412